# George de Hevesy
## *LIFE AND WORK*

Publication of this biography was sponsored by
the George de Hevesy Foundation, Zürich, Switzerland
and
General Electric Nuclear Medical A/S, Copenhagen,
Denmark.

# George de Hevesy

## LIFE AND WORK

*A Biography*
*by*
*Hilde Levi*

With compliments

*To*
*Sophie Hellman*
*who shared my experience of*
*Hevesy and the Niels Bohr Institute*
*for many years*

George de Hevesy
LIFE AND WORK
© Hilde Levi/Rhodos, Copenhagen 1985

ISBN: 87 7245 054 1
Printed in Denmark

# Contents

# Preface

In the 20th century the advancement of the sciences and of technology has accelerated so tremendously that discoveries and progress made in the first half appeared trivial and were taken for granted in the second half of our century. The people who had the ingenious ideas, and their efforts to realize them, are soon forgotten and we rush on with ever increasing haste. The competitive drive so characteristic of present day research leaves little time for retrospect, much less for thought about the benefits versus the risks – or the losses – resulting from all these efforts.

However, some counter-weight to this pushing ahead can be seen in the growing interest in the history of scientific developments and the personalities who brought them about. The history of science is an expanding field which has lately gained recognition. This may be due in part to the fact that we have seen so much valuable documentation being irretrievably lost. At the same time, the manner in which research is being conducted now is quite different from that of a few decades ago: the individual yields to teamwork and the written word is bypassed by telecommunication. Letter-writing as a means of exchanging ideas and information has become obsolete.

George Hevesy, Hungarian born but a resident of many lands, was one of the great individualists and diligent correspondents of the 20th century. His contributions to many branches of science were far-reaching. His influence spanned over half a century and brought him into close contact with many other men of science all over the world. But the story of his life remained fairly unknown.

I had the good fortune to be his assistant and co-worker in Copenhagen for a decade (1934-43), and our close scientific contact lasted until 1950 when Hevesy settled permanently in Sweden. There his work focused on topics quite different from those studied by his former associates in Denmark. However, we met repeatedly until the last years of his life.

On several occasions I have described his personality and my experiences as his co-worker, but I always felt that I did not know and understand him well enough to write his biography. This situation changed when – after my retirement – I began to work with Hevesy's scientific legacy which is deposited at the Niels Bohr Archive in Copenhagen. Letters, notes, and manuscripts provided a key to where one might search for additional material. This search gave ample results. The collection now contains much scientific as well as biographic information of interest, which is not immediately relevant to the present study. It is to be hoped that researchers in the history of science – and of the humanities – will avail themselves of this treasure.

The present biography of George Hevesy as a personality is based mainly on hundreds of letters Hevesy wrote to some of his contemporaries between 1911 and 1966. His correspondence is a good example of the unique value of the art of letter writing. From the factual information contained in the letters, the very style of the correspondence, and the impressions I had gained during thirty years of personal acquaintance emerged a picture of a great scientist who was able to overcome many adversities as well as personal conflicts through his intellectual strength and his optimism, but who kept his private life to himself.

This biography does not aim at presenting or evaluating in detail Hevesy's innumerable scientific endeavours and achievements. After reading his letters I became fascinated primarily by his complex personality and therefore want to describe – as best I can – the man in his time rather than his many research projects. Hevesy was a prolific writer who, in addition to several hundred original scientific papers, published a large number of survey articles and books. From the bibliography given in the appendix the reader can choose the topics that are of special interest to him. Hevesy has presented most of them also in a semi-popular form. Hence, there seems little reason to repeat what he – and others – already have explained and discussed several times.

I am most grateful to all who have given me access to Hevesy's correspondence. My sincere thanks are due to Miss Eva Paneth, London, daughter of the late F. A. Paneth, for the permission to study and to quote from the extensive correspondence between her father and Hevesy, which is now deposited in the Archive of the Max Planck Gesellschaft in Berlin. This collection comprises about 800 letters from the years 1912-58, and it has been the most elucidating source of information for this biography. I am also grateful to Professor B. Karlik, Vienna, who provided copies of Hevesy's correspondence with Stefan Meyer, the founder of the Vienna Radium Institute. Dr. Ch. Huggins of the University of Chicago U.S.A. has generously placed his collection of letters from Hevesy at my disposal. The complete Hevesy-Huggins correspondence gives a moving picture of the last ten years of Hevesy's life. In addition, the Niels Bohr Archive provided the letters written to and by Niels Bohr, and the Cambridge University Library kindly placed Hevesy's letters to Rutherford at my disposal.

This large Hevesy collection contains letters written in English, German, and the Scandinavian languages. Hevesy spoke all of them fluently, but none of them idiomatically, which is also evident in his writing. Therefore, his expressions are often odd and at the same time charming and always characteristic of his personality. I have chosen to quote from his writings in German and English without any corrections, and to provide translations into English of the German letters. Rather than rendering his German in idiomatic English, I have tried to retain some of his own wording and hence his personal style. Danish letters are given in English only.

My efforts to make the portrait of Hevesy as truthful and objective as possible and to describe the circumstances and historical events that shaped his life needed the support of knowledgable colleagues. Professor H. Holter has been my sternest and also most understanding critic. Thanks to his personal experience of the political and cultural trends during the Habsburg epoch, he could comment on many aspects of Hevesy's background and early development. He also knew Hevesy personally in the 1930ies by way of scientific contacts. I am truly grateful for his guidance.

Innumerable discussions with Finn Aaserud, p.t. a doctoral fellow in the history of science at the Niels Bohr Institute, and his generosity in letting me take advantage of his large collection of historical documents, have been most helpful. I wish to express my appreciation of our good comradeship.

I am grateful to Professor Aage Bohr who, at an early stage of my work, suggested that I write this essay and gave me access to the Niels Bohr Archive and its facilities. Last but not least, I am greatly indebted to Hevesy's children, especially his oldest daughter Jenny and her husband, Dr. Gustaf Arrhenius, for several conversations and valuable comments. Also George de Hevesy jun. and Ingrid de Hevesy-Rådman were very cooperative. Many illustrations reproduced in the biography were kindly placed at my disposal by the Hevesy family, by Professor Karlik, Miss Paneth, and the Niels Bohr Archive.

*Hilde Levi*

George de Hevesy, ca. 1960.

# Family Background and Youth

George Hevesy hardly ever spoke or wrote about his family background, his childhood or youth. Not until his old age did he refer in a more personal style to his experiences as a young man, but even these late reminiscences deal almost exclusively with his contemporaries, fellow scientists and their achievements, and tell very little about Hevesy's own life. At the height of his career he published a collection of what he considered his hitherto most important biological papers and introduced these volumes with some autobiographical sketches which he also published elsewhere (cf. reference p. 122). There he gives some of the highlights of his life – first of all encounters with the great personalities of his time – as he saw them at that moment.

Even his children heard very little about their father's background except that the family owned large estates in Hungary. Their grandfather died in 1920 and their grandmother in 1931; only the oldest of Hevesy's children remembers her grandmother and visits in her stately home, Tapio-Szap the ancestral estate. During an interview that took place in 1981 Hevesy's only surviving brother Paul, a professional diplomat trained under the Habsburg dynasty, and a representative of his native country for many years, recalled his youth as a very happy one in the strict and fairly regimented style of the epoch.

Thus, information about George Hevesy's ancestors and family background comes mainly from sources outside his own family circle (ref. p. 122). Both his parents were descendents of Jewish families who had lived in Hungary for several generations and had acquired prominence and wealth in the early 19th century. The father, Lajos Bischitz was the son of a merchant in Pest who had leased one of the large Esterhazy estates.

Hevesy's paternal grandmother came from the well known Hungarian bourgeois Fischer family, she had played a prominent role as the founder of a Jewish ladies' society and had initiated a Jewish charity in Pest. Hevesy's mother, the baroness Eugenie Schossberger de Tornya came from a very wealthy Jewish family who was involved in the oil and tobacco business; Hevesy's maternal grandfather, S. V. Schossberger, also became the chairman of the Jewish community of Pest, a post to which he was appointed by the Kaiser. Following tradition, his loyalty to the Habsburgs was even greater than that to the Magyar nobility; nevertheless, he was the first non-converted Jew to become a Magyar nobleman in 1863. By that time he was also one of the biggest Jewish landowners in the country.

Towards the end of the century, the Schossbergers were so influential that they were appointed to a barony. Among other large companies they owned the mining enterprise in northern Hungary where Hevesy's father was a managing director, besides being on the board of several big companies and running his large estates.

The Bischitz family was ennobled in 1895 and allowed to take on the name Bisicz de Heves. From 1906 they called themselves Hevesi de Heves, and later just de Hevesy.

The Hevesys were a big family: 5 boys were born between 1877 and 1885. Then followed an intermission of almost 12 years until baroness Eugenie de Hevesy gave birth to three more children, all of them girls. In accordance with the life style of that period, the boys were brought up to enter a profession. All of them went to a catholic monastic school in Budapest run by the Piarists and thus, for a period of close to 10 years, were under the strong influence of the patres piarum scholarum, an order whose members are devoted to the education of youth. Clearly, the family was on the way to complete assimilation and wished to be integrated into the society of which they were a part; since the social elite in Budapest were Magyar, the traditional cultural links of the Jews with the Viennese educated upper class under the Habsburgs had somehow to be made compatible with the more agrarian elite of the Hungarian Magyars. The bridge between these groups had been established by way of the influence many Jewish families had gained through the administration of the large estates, traditionally in the hands of the Magyars.

The baroness Eugenie Schossberger de To-    G. Hevesy. Courtesy: the Hevesy family.
nya, G. Hevesy's mother, in the 1870s.
Courtesy: the Hevesy family.

Paul de Hevesy recalled that at the Piarist school, lessons started early in the morning and continued after the midday meal recess well into the afternoon. In addition, one or two private tutors who stayed with the family gave further instruction in German, English, and French. The main languages were spoken alternately for one day at a time, also at the dinner table and the private tutoring hours. Learning and studying thus being the main occupation, school and homework took up between 10 and 12 hours every day. In those days, Paul de Hevesy muses, children were expected to acquire a large body of knowledge, and had little time left for play and hobbies or sports.

The girls had a less rigorous schedule; they too went to a convent school and were taught to master several languages, but in general, the girls were brought up to get married, naturally to men of standing. They did not have to master more prosaic and practical aspects of housekeeping.

The influence of this monastic education is noticeable in George Hevesy's life and in his approach to many problems; it becomes evident towards the end of his life.

G. Hevesy's father, Mr. Lajos Bisicz de Heves. Courtesy: the Hevesy family.

G. Hevesy's paternal grandmother. Courtesy: the Hevesy family.

The oldest son of the Hevesys, Wilhelm, became an airplane engineer and explorer, the second son, André, was a writer, the third, Edmond, later took over the directorship of the mining business, the fourth, Paul, was trained as a diplomat – as already mentioned – and served as an ambassador of Austria-Hungary in many capitals of the world. None of the four brothers left an heir.

On leaving the school of the Holy Order of Joseph of Calazane, the youngest Hevesy son George broke away from the family traditions and decided to become a scientist. He began his studies at the University of Budapest but soon moved on to more advanced institutions of learning; he went to Berlin; he was most interested in chemistry. However, the climate of Berlin did not agree with him – so he himself reports; it seems that his health was rather frail already at that time, and remained so throughout his life. After half a year, he left Berlin in 1905 for Freiburg im Breisgau, where the climate was much better.

Although his studies focused on physics and chemistry, Hevesy was fascinated by the great Austrian philosopher Ernst Mach and followed courses in philosophy and also some in biology. In 1906 he began to work for his doctoral thesis at Freiburg University under the physical chemist Georg Meyer, the topic being the interaction of metallic sodium with molten sodium hydroxide. Hevesy obtained his degree in the fall of 1908 at the age of 23.

There are no written records of any sort telling about Hevesy's nonscientific interests, his friends, or his way of life during his student years, – he never tells about that period in his autobiographical notes or in his letters, but he mentions that he sometimes invited friends to his father's estate for hunting parties. Since the neighbouring estate was Hungarian state property where the emperor Franz Joseph held many of his shooting parties, Hevesy's father often participated in these hunts and even young George was admitted once in a while. Throughout his long life, Hevesy felt a great love for nature, he loved to go for walks, and skiing was his great passion. In many of his letters to friends, the pleasure and strength he gained from watching a beautiful landscape is expressed in quite poetic language. Even when having to choose a place to live permanently or for an extended period of time – for example when he was offered a professorship later in his career – the environment and climate of the place was as important a factor as its scientific potential.

After Hevesy had concluded his studies and received his Ph.D. from the University of Freiburg, he went to Zürich to work under Richard Lorenz. He later recalled that there were a number of learned men at this institute so he could catch up on several subjects he had not fully assimilated in Freiburg. He met Richard Willstätter who was head of the chemistry department. The following year (1909) Albert Einstein came to Zürich; he was rather unknown at that time, but Hevesy was among the few who attended his inaugural lecture.

When Lorenz accepted a chair at the University of Frankfurt/M, Hevesy could have stayed on in Zürich and was encouraged to do so by Willstätter, but he preferred to work for some time with Fritz Haber in Karlsruhe, whose field of interest was close to his own. He went to Karlsruhe, but it soon turned out that Haber's and Hevesy's interests did not match too well. Moreover, Haber, who was the bossy type of a German professor, wanted to study electron emission during the oxida-

G. Hevesy's mother. Courtesy: the Hevesy family.

G. Hevesy's father in court-dress of the Habsburg period. Courtesy: the Hevesy family.

One of the family residences. Courtesy: the Hevesy family.

G. Hevesy in the laboratory at Freiburg ca. 1907. Courtesy: the Hevesy family.

tion of liquid Na-K alloys but did not master the technique required for this kind of work. Hence, after only 3 months in Karlsruhe, Hevesy decided that he wanted to spend some time in Manchester in order to learn the technique – and then return to Haber.

Early in Hevesy's life – he is only 25 years old – we notice some traits in his personality, which come to play important roles throughout his life. One is his restlessness, his strong inclination to move from place to place. Even later, in periods of relative stability, when he held the same position for several years, he was constantly on the go, travelling either for scientific reasons or in order to visit his homeland and family for whom he never stopped longing, or also to seek recuperation from his frequent illnesses. His poor health affected his working ability and hence his career and also his life style to an increasing degree as he grew older.

This strong urge to travel and see people and places could be satisfied in his younger years thanks to the family's wealth. Hevesy did not have to look for a job in order to make a living; he could choose and pursue his postgraduate training wherever he expected his scientific interests to be met and promoted. When he asked Ernest Rutherford in 1910 for permission to work in his Manchester laboratory, the financing of his stay was not even mentioned. Rutherford agreed to accept him, however, on the condition that he stay and work for a year. Hevesy would be admitted as a research student, would have to pay his fee, but laboratory facilities would be free.

Dear Sir,                                                                      June 25, 1910
I have received your letter asking permission to work at the Physical Laboratory of the University of Manchester on Radioactivity.
I shall be pleased to consider favourably your proposal provided you are able to spend at least a University year in the Laboratory. Some little time is required to become acquainted with the methods of measurement and it is not possible to hope to accomplish even short research under that period.
I may mention for your guidance that you could probably be admitted as a "Research student". This entails a fee of £ 9-9-0 per year to the University and covers the greater part of the University expenses. The Laboratory provides all the apparatus and facilities for research free of charge.
I shall be glad to hear from you whether you will be able to come under these conditions.

Yours sincerely    E. Rutherford

June 25ᵗʰ 1910

Dear Sir

I have received your letter asking permission to work in the Physical Laboratory of the University of Manchester at Radioactivity.

I shall be pleased to consider favourably your proposal provided you are able to spend at least a University year in the Laboratory. Some

little time is required to become acquainted with the methods of measurement and it is not possible to hope to accomplish even a short research under that period.

21

I may mention
for your guidance that
you could probably
be admitted as
a "Research Student".
This entails a fee of
£9-9-0 per year to the
University & covers the
greater part of your the
University expenses. The
laboratory furnishes all
necessary apparatus
& facilities *for research* free of charge.

I shall be glad
to hear from you
whether you will
be able to come
under these conditions.

Yours sincerely
E Rutherford

Dr G von Hevesy
Karlsruhe.

22

# Beginning of an Academic Career in Manchester and Vienna

Hevesy's move to Manchester was delayed because of health problems. Illness prevented him from travelling to Manchester soon after he had been accepted, and Rutherford advised him to avoid the severe winter in Manchester and to wait till after Christmas. When Hevesy finally crossed the Channel in January 1911, he became so seasick that he spent several weeks in bed in London before he could begin his work.

Unfortunately, there is no first hand record of the decisive year 1911 in Hevesy's career. The only source of information is a number of reminiscences he wrote much later. Hevesy started his work as he had planned, familiarizing himself with the technique of radioactivity measurements. Rutherford suggested that he determine the solubility of actinium emanation in water, and since this radioactive substance has a half-life of only 4 seconds, this was a tricky problem. Somewhat later Rutherford suggested another task – even more complex than the first – namely to separate radium-D from the huge amount of lead in pitchblende he had obtained from the uranium mines in Joachimsthal, Bohemia. This story has been told so many times and on many occasions by Hevesy himself that it has become one of the basic anecdotes of classical radioactivity. In his autobiographical notes for example, he reports that Rutherford said "My boy if you are worth your salt you will separate the RaD from all that nuisance of lead". After lengthy trials Hevesy realized that a separation was impossible. His efforts failed completely. In his notes he continues "to make the best of this depressing situation, I thought to avail myself of the fact that RaD is inseparable from lead, and to label small amounts of lead by addition of RaD obtained from tubes in which radium emanation decayed".

23

Hevesy's failure to separate these "chemically identical" elements and the conclusions he drew from his negative results became the turning point of his scientific career and the basis for his most significant contribution to science: namely, the use of radioactive isotopes as tracers. The events and ideas of this period were the focal point to which he returned time and again, although his scientific interest during several periods seemed to lead him in other directions. He was so preoccupied with his new tasks that he had lost all interest in the problems Haber had suggested and had no intention to return to Karlsruhe.

Aside from the immense influence of Rutherford and his school on the scientific career of the young Hevesy, one can hardly overestimate the imprint they made on Hevesy's personal development. Rutherford's personality and his approach to scientific as well as to personal and political questions put his stamp on his co-workers, many of whom were – or grew to become – outstanding scientists and very special characters. They all contributed to the shaping of the young Hevesy. Of greatest importance and of far reaching consequence was the friendship with Niels Bohr who came to Manchester in 1912. From their first meeting Hevesy was deeply impressed with Bohr and he has described their first encounter, their relationship during the following years, and their lasting friendship innumerable times both in his autobiographical notes and especially, towards the end of his life, in his letters to friends and colleagues. As both men grew old (they were of the same age) these reminiscences found moving expression in several letters they exchanged.

In the early Manchester days, Hevesy and Bohr shared the same problems and difficulties arising from being strangers in a country and among people whose language they did not master too well; they had to adapt to a new milieu and to a demanding, older, fairly authoritarian professor. They were preoccupied with new and not yet clarified ideas. Although their cultural backgrounds and scientific orientations were very different – or maybe just because of this difference – they established a personal friendship which lasted a lifetime. At that time the Manchester laboratory was a scientific center and Rutherford gathered around him a large group of talented younger scientists both from England and from abroad who came to play an important part in the following decades of

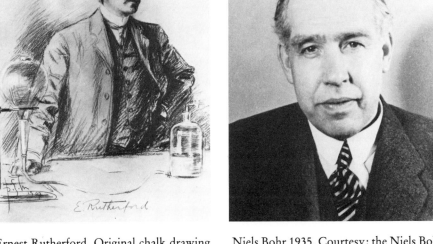

Ernest Rutherford. Original chalk drawing at Mc Gile University, Canada. Courtesy: the Niels Bohr Archive.

Niels Bohr 1935. Courtesy: the Niels Bohr Archive.

physical and chemical research. This situation repeated itself in some ways two decades later as Rutherford aged and Bohr approached his most influential period, attracting in turn the most brilliant young researchers from all over the world to his institute in Copenhagen.

During this first year, Hevesy did stay in Manchester as Rutherford had requested; and after this apprenticeship, he was well versed in atomic physics. This was the time when the atomic nucleus was discovered and the nature and origin of ionizing radiation was understood. The term "isotope", however, had not been coined; it had become clear that substances – or elements – exist which are chemically inseparable and might be called chemically identical, although their atomic weights were found to be different. In several countries, scientists struggled to identify the decay products of the radioactive elements, and to understand the relationship between the emission of different types of radiation and the change in "identity" of these products, i.e. their position in the periodic table.

Needless to say, besides co-operation there was at times rather hard competition between individuals and also strong ambitions with national

25

overtones in these attempts at understanding the large body of discon-
nected information which became available in the field of radioactivity and
atomic physics. Rutherford was not only the highest authority, he was the
arbitrator between competing hotheads. Also Hevesy was exceedingly
eager to contribute to the clarification of these problems with his own
experimental results. During his first year in Manchester he made use of his
physico-chemical training, for example studying solubility and the elec-
tro-chemistry of the radio-elements; he also became involved in an
investigation of valency changes and of the new position in the periodic
table an element occupied after the emission of radiation. The rules
describing these processes were called the "displacement law".

By the end of 1911, Hevesy was exhausted and had lost weight. He
returned to Hungary – albeit visiting people and places on the way – and
later spent many weeks in a nursing home outside Graz in Austria. From
there he went vacationing together with his family on the Adriatic coast.
During this period, he corresponded frequently with Rutherford, who
made his influence felt in order to speed the publication of Hevesy's
papers. On his way from England, Hevesy had paid a visit to Kasimir
Fajans in Karlsruhe who worked on the displacement law; and from there
he proceeded to Vienna in order to have a look at the Radium Institute
which had been founded in 1910. The young Hevesy, after less than one
year with Rutherford, felt quite superior on behalf of the Manchester
laboratory, telling Rutherford in a letter dated 14 February 1912 that in
Vienna they had plenty of room and a lot of new apparatus; he continued
"If the latter and a lot of radium would be sufficient to make important
discoveries, they should make them. Unfortunately, it does not seem to be
the case". In view of the fact that the head of the Vienna Institute,
Professor Stefan Meyer was 13 years his senior and one of the outstanding
pioneers in that period's research in the field of radioactivity, Hevesy's
report to Rutherford can be understood not only as an expression of
youthful enthusiasm for Manchester, but at the same time as an early signal
of another characteristic trait of Hevesy's personality, which became very
strong as the years went by: Hevesy was quick to evaluate people, their
work, their actions, and he had no doubt that his judgement was correct
and final. Thus, already when he was a young man, his self-confidence was

very great. This characteristic is exceedingly evident as Hevesy becomes a recognized and highly esteemed scientist; it is expressed often and clearly in his later correspondence.

In late spring of 1912, after he had recuperated, Hevesy returned to Manchester. It is not quite clear exactly when Rutherford asked him to separate RaD "from all that nuisance of lead". Evidently these efforts were begun in 1911 and continued the following year. In a letter dated 4 February 1912, Hevesy wrote to Rutherford "In the Viennese laboratory somebody is working since a long time on the same subject. I have not mentioned it to Professor Meyer that we try also the separation". Hevesy's reaction illustrates the competition among the young scientists mentioned above. As he explained much later Hevesy tried to turn his failure with this project into a success by devising an application of his negative result. He had the idea that radioactive elements which are chemically inseparable from non-radioactive ones could be used as "indicators" for the latter. He showed that it had become possible by means of radioactivity measurements to study chemical processes which could not be observed in any other way. For example: It is impossible to study ordinary lead, or lead salts, diffusing in or exchanging with solid lead because the Pb atoms originating in the salt cannot be distinguished from those present in the solid lead. However, if the lead atoms in the salt emit radiation – RaD being radioactive, but chemically identical with ordinary lead – then the radioactive lead atoms originating in the salt can be distinguished from the ordinary ones in the solid metal, and their movement – diffusion or exchange – can be observed. Hevesy actually performed many experiments of this type. These investigations and the application of the indicator technique that became possible about 20 years later, are Hevesy's most outstanding contribution to science. He expanded, refined, and varied this method throughout the active period of his life.

Late in 1912 Hevesy returned to Hungary, mainly to obtain his "Habilitation" or "venia legendi" i.e. the right to establish himself as a teacher and to give lectures at the university. As usual, he did some visiting on the way. In the meantime, the Vienna Radium Institute had aroused his special interest, so he stopped there again and was shown around by Stefan Meyer who told him that his young co-worker Fritz Paneth had

27

Fritz A. Paneth in the 1950s. Courtesy: Miss Eva Paneth.

Stefan Meyer, director of the Vienna Radium Institute. Courtesy: the Vienna Institute.

made unsuccessful efforts to separate RaD from lead. A few weeks later, Hevesy wrote to Paneth from Budapest, regretting that they had not met, and suggesting that they set out on a co-operation. Paneth's reaction was positive and he proposed a topic which, however, was not what interested Hevesy. In response Hevesy wrote to Paneth on 8 January 1913 "... as such I like to suggest to you the following: Since RaD cannot be separated from lead we can take RaD as an indicator for lead and, for example, investigate the solubility of $PbCrO_4$ (lead chromate) in water at different temperatures."[*] Paneth agreed to work on this problem. During the spring of 1913 Hevesy went back and forth between Budapest and Vienna and at the same time prepared himself for his Habilitation lecture "On the constitution of the atoms and the properties of the electron" – as he explained in a letter to Rutherford on 3 January 1913. He also mentioned

[*]*8 January 1913 to Paneth*
"... möchte ich Ihnen folgendes vorschlagen: Da sich das RaD vom Blei nicht trennen lässt, können wir RaD als Indikator des Bleis nehmen und zum Beispiel die Löslichkeit des $PbCrO_4$ in Wasser bei verschiedenen Temperaturen untersuchen".

that he "had a few weeks to spare" which he used, together with Paneth, to study solubility and diffusion of lead salts and to continue his earlier work on the separation of RaD from lead. The most important topic, however, was the development of the more general and widely applicable idea of using radio-elements as indicators in analytical chemistry.

The collaboration with Paneth was indeed exceedingly productive scientifically as well as intellectually, resulting in 6 papers. The sequence of names on these publications alternated because they agreed that the basic idea was conceived by both of them independently and simultaneously. During this brief period, Hevesy became very much attached to the Radium Institute and its staff. Not unlike Rutherford's institute, the Vienna institute under the leadership of Stefan Meyer attracted many gifted young co-workers and, over many years from the beginning of the century, this group made important contributions to the understanding of radioactivity and ionizing radiation. The life style in Vienna was in tune with the relaxed, nonchalant Austrian laissez-faire atmosphere, the scientific staff being knit together through a number of family relations, definitely in a less formal and also less authoritarian style than that prevailing in Manchester.

Hevesy's friendship with Paneth lasted until the latter's death 46 years later, and so did the very warm relationship with Stefan Meyer for whom Hevesy retained great respect and veneration. In the years to come, Paneth exerted considerable influence on Hevesy as regards the way in which scientific experiments should be carried out and papers be written. Hevesy continued to be the driving force, and Paneth was the patient painstaking worker who wanted everything done correctly and conscientiously.

While working in Vienna, early in 1913, Hevesy corresponded frequently with Rutherford, reporting on the progress he made together with Paneth and on the work of other institute members. On 28 February, he wrote "With the exception of yourself everybody whom I spoke about the Vienna laboratory had a poor opinion of this place. I must say this opinion is wrong, the work of those who sacrifice themselves by doing less interesting work with great accuracy for the benefit of all of us, should be estimated very highly." This remark is very typical of Hevesy; he never was prepared to do "less interesting work" and great accuracy was not his hallmark. Apart from the discussion of scientific topics and his eagerness to have his results published speedily – preferably both in England and in Germany – the Rutherford-Hevesy correspondence of the pre-war period touches repeatedly on political questions which, naturally, were on everybody's mind and caused considerable concern.

The political situation in Europe and the Balkan States was one of confrontation and shifting alliances between the big powers: England, France, Russia, and the smaller countries alike. Germany and Austria had formed an alliance which Italy later joined and, as a counter-move, France and Russia became allies. Then Britain came to an agreement with France (1904) and later with Russia (1907) forming an "entente" which aimed at isolating Germany. In the Balkan States, the conflict arising from the geographical location of a multitude of small countries versus the disarray of different ethnic groups across seemingly arbitrary borders, was one of the important factors which made the political situation in south eastern Europe very unstable. Another one was the Turkish dominance of the region. In 1912 some of the Christian states went to war against the Turks. The peace treaty of 1913 forced the Turks to retreat to Adrianople. Even before these events, in 1908, Austria annexed Bosnia and Hercegowina from the Turks, and at about the same time Russia incited the Serbs against Austria, and the Czechs sympathized with this development. Among the various Balkan States, conflicts arose and wars were being fought and during this period the Pan-Slavist movement grew in strength. In the following years, the Austro-Hungarian empire, with the tacit support of Germany, continued a dominant and aggressive policy towards the Balkan States and thereby stimulated the Pan-Slavist movement and its allegiance with Russia. The murder in Sarajevo was the trigger that started the First World War.

In his letters to Rutherford Hevesy described at some length the tension between the Austro-Hungarian dynasty's dominance over the "bellicose" Balkan States and, as is to be expected, he expressed his loyalty to the Habsburgs and his patriotism; he scorned the political conflicts in central Europe. Rutherford, although born in New Zealand, had the typically British calm and reasonable approach to the crisis, and could not really conceive that people would be so foolish as to go to war over these quarrels

(14 December 1912). Several years later the remembrance of this friendly exchange between the mature Britisher and the young Hungarian may well have lingered in Rutherford's mind when he was hesitant – soon after the end of the war – to welcome Hevesy back to Manchester.

Hevesy concluded his work at the Vienna Institute in March, and after a travel and vacation period, he returned to Manchester late in May 1913 and stayed until September. In the meantime Paneth had come to England on a fellowship and was working in Glasgow. They met and corresponded frequently, exchanging ideas and the results of their experiments, which were published in a series of papers.

The winter of 1913-14, more precisely from October 1913 through March 1914, was the first and only extended period Hevesy spent working as a scientist at the University of Budapest. He had modest laboratory facilities at the chemistry department, began purchasing a few instruments in order to be able to measure alpha and beta rays, and he obtained some uranium and radio-thorium from Stefan Meyer and also from Otto Hahn who worked in Berlin, respectively. However, it turned out more difficult to establish a laboratory than he had anticipated and his experimental work progressed very slowly, thus giving him time for theoretical studies and for the completion of a number of papers together with Paneth. During this lonely and cumbersome period he realized that Paneth's very careful editing and proof-reading of their manuscripts was indispensable, and he named him his "Ober-Hof-Korrektur-Leser", a distinction Paneth retained throughout their many, many years of co-authorship. Almost in every letter to his friend, Hevesy expressed his longing for Vienna and his desire to do experiments together with his colleagues at the Radium Institute. But, although he kept announcing his immediate arrival in Vienna, the trip was delayed until June – in part because his poor health forced him to take a longer vacation in Meran, a popular resort town in Southern Tyrol.

Hevesy had planned to return to England in order to work with Henry G. J. Moseley whom he had met in Rutherford's laboratory in Manchester. Moseley was one of the most promising co-workers there; he had accepted a post at the University of Oxford where he continued his work in X-ray spectroscopy. Hevesy considered this method to be so important

31

Fritz A. Paneth in his laboratory at the Vienna Radium Institute, ca. 1912. Courtesy: the Vienna Institute.

G. Hevesy during the Manchester period. Courtesy: the Hevesy family.

that he wanted to learn it. On his way via Prague and Berlin, he was invited to speak about the new concept of "isotopy" before Heinrich Rubens' colloquium in Berlin. In the course of a few days in Berlin, he discussed the confusing multitude of new ideas he had on his mind – primarily the concept of "chemical identity" – with members of different research groups at the Kaiser Wilhelm Institute, the Reichsanstalt, and the University. In the evenings, he wrote long reports on these discussions to Paneth, describing his excitement especially with Walther Nernst who was known to be very critical and disbelieving in matters of "isotopy". But finally, after many hours of talk, Hevesy reported how he succeeded in convincing Nernst that the atomic number rather than the atomic weight determines the chemical properties of an element. In his letter to Paneth of 16 July 1914 he ends the story with the sentence "how strange, for a friend of Bohr and Moseley nothing could be closer than this idea, but here in Berlin they are no Bohr enthusiasts and they are not very knowledgeable about the problem of atomic number."[*] It took only a few years to change this situation dramatically: until Bohr came to Berlin in 1920 in order to discuss the atomic theory.

In a state of intellectual elation, Hevesy left Berlin for Scheveningen where he planned to spend a week before proceeding to Oxford. But – this was not to be: the war broke out on August 1 before he had left Holland. On August 2 he wrote to Paneth "The re-valuation of all values has occurred. Who can be interested now in whether or not isotopes can replace each other completely."** Although he was truly shaken and overwhelmed by the war situation, Hevesy's thoughts quickly returned to his scientific problems: his letter to Paneth continued in the usual style and he explained that he would make use of the library in Amsterdam in case he should be delayed in Holland for any length of time. A few days later, Hevesy met with his sister who had been visiting England and together they travelled homeward, reaching the resort town of Karlsbad later in August. He was never again to see Moseley who was killed in 1915 in the battle of the Dardanelles.

*16 July 1914 to Paneth
"wie merkwürdig, einem Freunde von Bohr und Moseley liegt nichts näher als dieser Gedanke, aber hier in Berlin ist man kein Bohr-Enthusiast und auch nicht sehr im Klaren mit diesen Problemen der Atomzahl".

**2 August 1914 to Paneth
"Die Umwertung aller Werte ist eingetreten. Wen interessiert es jetzt ob die Isotope sich völlig vertreten oder nicht".

# First World War

The outbreak of the First World War brought Hevesy to a crossroad in his life and career because the political and social order in Europe changed drastically and thus affected his life style and his future professional possibilities. In the first weeks, he fell victim to the contagious enthusiasm and patriotism around him; he wrote Paneth that he wanted to enlist as a volunteer together with all his friends. However, this enthusiasm cooled pretty soon. Like many among the privileged, he had the illusion that these events might develop into an ordeal for many but not really for him, and that the familiar life style could be maintained or – at least soon – be re-established. He postponed his enlistment till the last minute, that is until June 1915 when further delay would have brought him into trouble with the military authorities.

During the years that followed, his cherished freedom of movement and of choosing his own working conditions were entirely lost. Between September 1914 and May 1915, although restricted to visiting Vienna from Budapest, he still could continue his research with Paneth, and they managed to publish a surprising number of papers in German and Austrian journals. They applied the indicator method to studies of the physico-chemical properties of heavy metals and their inorganic salts. Since his activities were limited and he had little contact with scientists in other countries, he directed his urge to be active towards writing up their results in several versions. This habit actually stayed with him in later years, especially after the writing of scientific papers and reports had become a routine which did not cause him any headache.

In the early summer of 1915, Hevesy somewhat reluctantly joined the ranks of the "K. and K. Austrio-Hungarian army", and his experience there was catastrophic. He could not endure the first strenuous march but collapsed and – unconscious and utterly exhausted – he had to be hospitalized. It took him weeks to recover. In a letter to Paneth of 29 June 1915 he explained that the head of the military hospital had examined him more thoroughly than any of his previous doctors had done, and diagnosed an "atony with a lowering of the stomach and acid dyspepsia and neurastenia". There was no question that Hevesy was unfit for active military service and had to be transferred to civil duties. In August 1915 he was ordered to become an apprentice in the X-ray unit of a Budapest hospital, a job he held until the following summer. It gave him a good deal of freedom to visit Vienna once in a while and to pursue his scientific interests. A priority quarrel with Fajans about the concept of chemical identity of isotopes, the properties of radio-elements, and their place in the periodic system dominated both his thoughts and his correspondence with Paneth and Stefan Meyer. In the summer of 1916, Hevesy was transferred to an electrolysis plant in Nagyteteny, not far from Budapest, with the special task of getting this factory to function properly and to melt old church bells from the Balkan countries in order to produce copper for military use. Hevesy did not like to carry out this task: he kept a piece of a church bell showing the Virgin and Child in relief and cherished this "souvenir" all his life. The organization of the factory caused him a lot of difficulties but he did get it to work and as soon as everything ran smoothly, he found time to resume some research. Hevesy often travelled to Budapest in order to stay in touch with fellow scientists, most of them likewise engaged in war projects. Especially his frequent meetings and discussions with his colleague Michael Polanyi helped to keep up his spirits in spite of recurrent health problems and the mounting difficulties due to shortage of food and, first of all, coal for heating purposes during the winter 1916-17.

In the summer of 1917, Hevesy proposed to Paneth that they join forces and write a small book about radioactivity. They discussed which topics should be included and also, how to divide various subjects between them. As usual, Hevesy was convinced that this would be a small task that could be managed within a short time, while Paneth was more reluctant; he was busy with his research in Vienna and also a teaching job in Prague, which later turned into a professorship. In principle, they agreed to embark on

35

Corporal G. Hevesy ca. 1915. Courtesy: the Vienna Institute.

this project, and Hevesy, whose daily duties were not very demanding and who had little else to pass the time with, immediately began to draft one chapter after the other. He did that without ready access to a library or other source material except what was stored in his excellent memory.

In the fall of 1917 Hevesy was suddenly transferred to the copper works in Beszterczebanya in northern Hungary, a small and idyllic town, almost 11 hours by train from Budapest. There he led a very quiet and lonely life, devoting a lot of time to writing the book. Hevesy was negotiating with a publisher although Paneth had not even started to write, which exacerbated Hevesy's impatience. By January 1918, he informed his friend that his part was finished – albeit as a draft which needed to be read by critical experts who were willing to do a thorough job of correcting. On 8 November 1918 he wrote: "Maybe you could give some chapters to Lawson to read, because he will probably soon travel home ... I definitely value Bohr's system of showing a manuscript to as many experts as possible, and I expect that those concerned not only have the proper understanding of the matter but also that they read the manuscript conscientiously."[*] Needless to say, the conscientious Paneth would need considerably more time to write his part, and hence the two authors were quite out of phase at this stage of the project.

Early in 1918 Hevesy learnt that the University of Pressburg planned to enlarge its faculty and offered several professorships. At that time Pressburg still was an Hungarian town – but only for one more year. In 1919 it became the capital of Slovakia, Bratislava. He was exceedingly interested in the chemistry professorship and asked both Richard Lorenz and Stefan Meyer to write recommendations. Stefan Meyer turned to Paneth for assistance, and together they composed a document, Hevesy acknowledged as being almost poetic and subtle in its wording. To his great disappointment, Hevesy did not get this position – his friend and colleague Gyula Groh was chosen instead – and he realized that this may have been the last chance for a scientific post in Hungary. In this context he

<hr>

*8 November 1918 to Paneth
"ich schätze durchaus Bohr's System Manuskripte möglichst vielen Sachkündigen zu zeigen, wobei ich allerdings voraussetze, dass die Betreffenden nicht nur Verständnis für die Sache haben sondern das Manuskript auch gewissenhaft durchsehen".

mentions for the first time the possibility that he might have to emigrate because there would be no opening for him in his own country. In a letter to Paneth of 23 April 1918 he says: "If I do not get this chair in Pozsony I probably have no other choice after the war but to emigrate.".*

In spite of a few short trips to Budapest and Vienna and his frequent contact with Paneth, life in Beszterczebanya was very lonely and Hevesy felt entirely isolated. On one of his trips, he had packed some instruments which he took along, and Stefan Meyer later sent him a thorium sample so that he could make a few rather primitive experiments in his "laboratory" at the factory. But this was not the kind of life that could satisfy his appetite for scientific activity. He embarked on writing an article for Graetz' "Handbuch der Elektrizität und des Magnetismus", which appeared in 1919 entitled "Elektrolyse und elektrolytische Polarisation". Although this was much more work than he had anticipated, it was more or less a pastime – "true" research was paralyzed. The cold winter of 1917-18 and the months that followed were one drawn-out pain for Hevesy. Shortage of food and coal and his isolation far away from Budapest contributed to a deterioration of his health. He suffered from recurring colds and influenza, he was discouraged. When the war ended in November, he was ordered back to Budapest but was not released from military service. The Czechs occupied Beszterczebanya, and Hevesy was afraid that he would lose all his belongings including Stefan Meyer's precious thorium sample which he had left behind. Luckily, this did not happen and the sample was returned to Vienna later. The increasingly chaotic political situation in most of Europe and the overthrow of the old social order made it impossible to plan for the future. In Budapest, the relatively democratic and liberal Count Károlyi had become prime minister, King Charles of Habsburg had abdicated and Hungary became a republic. Suddenly, Hungary was separated from Austria by closed borders, railroads did not function and mail was censored. For the restless and jobless Hevesy this was an almost unbearable situation.

*23 April 1918 to Paneth
"Bekomme ich den Lehrstuhl in Pozsony nicht, so bleibt mir nach dem Krieg wahrscheinlich nichts anderes übrig als aus zu wandern".

But fortunately, in the beginning of 1919 he was offered a position to act as a substitute over a period of one year for the ailing professor of the second Physical Institute at the University of Budapest. It meant that he had to concentrate on physics at the expense of his much greater interest in physical chemistry and his obligations towards the Graetz Handbook. He was supposed to give lectures and later to organize an experimental course for the students. However, the political situation soon underwent another drastic change: Károlyi was forced to resign, and the strongly communist and pro-Russian Béla Kun proclaimed Hungary a Soviet Republic. Although the Hungarian people supported Béla Kun who promised reforms which were badly needed, the new regime met with enormous difficulties also from the world outside. The allies intended to force a new order on the whole Balkan region and would not tolerate a Bolshevik regime in Hungary. In the early summer of 1919, the Roumanians marched toward Budapest, and although a hastily assembled Hungarian army managed to drive them back, Béla Kun was forced to flee. A period of "white terror" and chaos followed when Admiral Horthy with his right-wing patriotic followers set out to reverse the reforms and the re-organization of the country, which Béla Kun had introduced.

Hevesy was not at ease in this situation. He felt the threat of losing the chance for a position and his family's properties and wealth. Hungary's borders were closed and he was again isolated from his friends in the western world. His letters to Stefan Meyer and Paneth bear witness to his despair and his efforts at least to bring some money to Austria so that he could sustain himself until he had found a position – providing he was able to leave the country. It had become fairly clear during the revolution that there was no future for Hevesy in Budapest for many years to come. On 2 March 1919 he wrote to his friend Niels Bohr in Copenhagen who had invited him already while they were together in Manchester. Bohr understood the signal and his reaction was encouraging: he suggested that Hevesy visit him in the country during the summer vacation.

On his way to Copenhagen in August 1919, Hevesy could revisit Vienna for the first time since the war had ended. As an Hungarian citizen he now needed a visa to enter his second scientific home: the Radium Institute.

Paneth had moved to Hamburg because an Austrian professor was no longer acceptable at the Czechoslovakian University of Prague.

There exists no record of the conversations between Bohr and Hevesy because Hevesy visited Paneth on the way back to Budapest and there was thus no need for letter writing; nobody else enjoyed his confidence as Paneth did. During this visit they finally had a chance to discuss the subjects of the book they had attempted to write together while the war kept them apart.

No doubt, Bohr understood Hevesy's desperate situation and he was willing to help as best he could. They agreed that Hevesy should return to Copenhagen in the spring of 1920 when Bohr's new institute – which was under construction – was to be opened. From a scientific point of view this was a unique chance for Hevesy. On the other hand, at this moment Bohr did not have much to offer as regards a more permanent position or salary. In his letters to Paneth (27 November 1919) and Stefan Meyer (7 October 1919), Hevesy stressed the uncertainty of the situation.

In Budapest, the new Horthy regime was exceedingly active and Hevesy described it in his letters (2 November 1919) as being worse than Béla Kun's regime. Previous nominations were reversed, prosecution and blackmail of those who were not immediate followers of the ruling party were common. Also antisemitism flourished more than before. Hevesy described this situation to his friends as follows: "The university remains closed, this time the masters are those who were dismissed by the previous regime; now they judge over life and death and all who do not suit them are dismissed one after the other. I do not want to be thrown out and have informed the dean that I am willing to supplement physics only on the condition that the faculty definitely wishes me to do so, and I have further left the direction of the institute to the assistants who substitute for me."*

*7 October 1919 to Stefan Meyer
"Die Universität bleibt geschlossen, diesmal sind diejenigen die Herrn, die die frühere Regime suspendierte, jetzt richten sie über Leben und Tod und schmeissen der Reihe nach die ihnen nicht passenden hinaus ... Ich empfand keine Lust mich hinaus werfen zu lassen und habe dem Dekan mitgeteilt, dass ich nur unter solchen Bedingungen weiter Physik zu supplieren geneigt bin, wenn das die Fakultät ausdrücklich wünscht und habe die Leitung des Instituts den mich vertretenden Assistenten weiter überlassen."

Gersonsvej 55, Hellerup.
Kopenhagen. 23-12-19.

My dear Hevesy,

We all thank you so much for your kind Christmas greetings and send in return our very heartiest wishes for a happy new year for you and your relations. We are all looking forward so much to seeing you here in the spring, and I hope we shall succeed in making your stay here a pleasant time for you.

With kindest regards from my wife and Christian and Hansemand and myself   yours ever
Niels Bohr.

Letter from Niels Bohr to Hevesy. Transcription on p. 123.

On 2 November 1919 Hevesy wrote to Paneth:

"Life at the university is hardly different from death, a re-opening before the spring is not planned. The present regime has learnt much from the communists: at that time one could get rid of one's competitors by denouncing them as counter-revolutionaries. Today they are stamped anonymously or even openly as sympathizers with the previous regime. All nominations made under the Károlyi era or later – that is to say since Oct. 1918 – have been reversed, which is basically justified. But that they also prosecute those who have been nominated or promoted is less so (justified). Even before that time I had been proposed by the faculty for the extra-ordinary professorship in physical chemistry, otherwise they would also have caused me unpleasantnesses, although I did not in fact take over the professorship but instead continued with supplementing physics. Incidentally I have asked that an investigation be carried out about me, because well-meaning faculty members have spread the news that I have travelled around at the expense of the State and that I received from the Räte-government one million Kroner for this purpose. Moreover that on the day of the overturn of communism, I fled – however, two contradictory rumours. By the way, as I wrote you already, I gave up the direction of the physics institute for numerous reasons: One because of the scandalous removal of deserving assistants for political reasons, further because I will not be named the permanent director anyhow, and finally because the future is so desolate that I feel no desire to connect my fate with that of the University of Budapest and Hungary."*

*2 November 1919 to Paneth
"Das Leben an der Universität ist vom Tode kaum verschieden, an eine Eröffnung vor dem Frühjahr wird garnicht gedacht Die jetzige Regime hat viel von den Kommunisten gelernt, damals konnte man seine Konkurrenten beseitigen indem man sie als Gegenrevolutionäre angab; heute stempelt man sie, anonymus oder auch offen, als mit der verflossenen Regime Sympathisierende. Alle Ernennungen, die unter der Aera Károlyi oder später, also seit dem Okt. 1918 erfolgt sind wurden rückgängig gemacht, was im Grunde genommen berechtigt ist, dass sie diejenigen aber auch verfolgen, die ernannt oder befördert worden sind schon weniger. Ich wurde noch vor dieser Zeit zum Extraordinariat für phys. Chemie von der Fakultät vorgeschlagen sonst hätten sie mir auch Unannehmlichkeiten gemacht, trotzdem dass ich die Professur gar nicht bekleidet habe sondern weiter Physik supplierte. Ich bat übrigens eine Untersuchung gegen mich einzuleiten, da wohlwollende Fakultätsmitglieder die Nachricht verbreiten, dass ich auf Staatskosten herumgereist bin und von der

And on 27 November 1919 Hevesy wrote to Paneth:

"My personal situation is as follows: The nomination to the professorship in physical chemistry – like every nomination dating not only from the communist time but also from the first revolutionary government (thus since the end of October 1918) – has been annulled; that I have been proposed by the legal authority does not change this situation at all.

The substitute professorship in physics which I held I gave up immediately after my return for several reasons I have already mentioned recently, but even as Privatdozent (assistant professor) I do no longer belong to the university because, without disciplinary proceedings or reasoning, the faculty has deleted me from the list of teachers. Actually, I am grateful for this since I shall leave Budapest more easily, which I intended to do – as already mentioned to you earlier. By the way, the spirit and the morale of prevailing conditions at this university are better characterized by these facts than by any detailed description. Moreover, my direct and indirect co-workers are all gone ...

Bohr has called me very warmly to work at his laboratory which is under construction, and I shall definitely not avoid to work next to this unique human being. How far my activities there will be lasting ones cannot be judged today, especially because the language, financial, and also climatic difficulties must not be underestimated. Therefore I shall at the same time look around *to see* whether I can settle (habilitieren) at a German university, preferably in an agreeable, quiet town... In case you should know of something suitable, I shall be obliged."*

Räteregierung 1 Million Kronen zu diesem Zweck erhalten haben soll!! ferner dass ich am Tage des Sturzes des Kommunismus geflüchtet sein soll – zwei allerdings widersprechende Gerüchte. – Übrigens, wie ich ja schon unlängst geschrieben habe legte ich die Leitung des Phys. Institutes nieder aus zahlreichen Gründen, einmal wegen der skandalösen Entfernung von verdienstvollen Assistenten aus politischen Gründen, dann weil ich so nicht zum endgültigen Leiter ernannt werden werde, und schliesslich weil die Zukunft derart trostlos ist, dass ich keine Lust empfinde mein Schicksal mit dem der Budapester Universität und Ungarn zu verbinden.."

*27 November 1919 to Paneth*
"Meine persönliche Lage ist die folgende: Die Ernennung zum Professor der Physikalichen Chemie ist wie jede Ernennung nicht nur der kommunistischen Zeit sondern auch die der ersten Revolutionsregierung (also seit Ende Oktober 1918) nichtig, dass ich von der legalen

4 Februar 1920. Hevesy repeats what he said on November 27, and says also

"This political childishness will stop, but poverty will remain. Therefore I have made the final decision already in the fall never again to hold a scientifically active position in Hungary. Copenhagen is ideal for me, I venerate Bohr as much as I value him. The only difficulty is this, that one can stay there permanently only if one earns all that one needs outside (outside Austria). With an annual income of for example 50.000 Austrian Kronen one is a complete beggar outside. At this point my permanent stay in Copenhagen will fail ...".*

Behörde dazu vorgeschlagen worden bin ändert an der Sachlage garnichts. Die stellvertretende Professur für Physik die ich innehatte legte ich sofort nach meiner Rückkehr nieder, aus verschiedenen, unlängst schon erwähnten Gründen, aber auch als Privatdozent gehöre ich der Universität nicht mehr an da mich die Fakultät ohne Disciplinarverfahren und ohne Begründung aus der Liste der Dozenten gestrichen hat. Ich bin ihr in letzter Linie dafür dankbar da ich umso leichter Budapest verlassen werde, das ich ja wie ich Dir ja erwähnt habe so und so vorhatte. Im übrigen wird Geist und Moral der Verhältnisse an der hiesigen Universität durch diese Tatsache besser charakterisiert als durch irgendwelche detaillierte Schilderung. Übrigens sind meine unmittelbare oder mittelbare Mitarbeiter so wie alle fort, ... Bohr hat mich sehr warm gerufen in seinem im Bau befindlichen Lab tätig zu sein und ich werde es sicher nicht vermeiden an der Seite dieses einzigartig dastehenden Menschen zu arbeiten. Wie weit meine dortige Tätigkeit eine dauernde sein wird lässt sich heute nicht übersehen zumal die sprachlichen, finanziellen und auch klimatischen Schwierigkeiten nicht zu unterschätzen sind. Ich werde mich also gleichzeitig umsehen ob ich mich an einer Deutschen Universität habilitieren kann, am liebsten in einer angenehmen, ruhigen Stadt. Solltest Du etwas passendes wissen, so wäre ich Dir dafür verbunden."

* 4 February 1920 to Paneth
"Die politischen Kindereien werden aufhören, aber die Armut wird uns bleiben, darum habe ich mich endgültig schon im Herbst entschlossen in Ungarn nie mehr eine wissenschaftliche Tätigkeit auszuüben.
  Kopenhagen ist für mich ideal, ich verehre Bohr ebenso hoch wie ich ihn schätze, die einzige Schwierigkeit liegt darin, dass man dort nur dann dauernd sich aufhalten kann wenn man alles was man braucht draussen verdient, mit einem jährlichen Einkommen von z.b. 50.000 öst. Kr. ist man ja draussen ein vollständiger Bettler. An diesem Punkt wird mein Verbleiben in Kopenhagen scheitern."

He then mentions a letter from Rutherford (mailed to Bohr on 13 January 1920).

"A few days ago I had a letter from Sir Ernest which pleased me very much. He writes: 'I shall, of course, be very glad to see you any time you come to Cambridge and to give you room if you wish to work in the laboratory, but I imagine it will be a year or two before such arrangements will be possible.' and this is what Bohr explained to me last summer."*

---

*Vor einigen Tagen hatte ich einen Brief von Sir Ernest der mir grosse Freude bereitete. Er schreibt under anderem: ....... Dieser Satz ist völlig im Einklang was mir Bohr im Letzten Sommer auseinandersetzte.

## First Copenhagen Period 1920-1926:
# The Discovery of Hafnium

In April 1920 Hevesy set out to begin a new chapter of his life in Copenhagen at Niels Bohr's Institute of Theoretical Physics. On the way from Budapest to Copenhagen he again visited several people and came also to Berlin where Bohr had been invited to lecture on his atomic theory. In Bohr's audience were all the great German physicists of that time, among them Planck and Einstein whom Bohr met for the first time on this occasion. The younger listeners present at these lectures felt that they did not have a chance to ask questions because the professors dominated the discussions. Therefore they persuaded Bohr to give them a special session from which full professors and bosses were excluded. This boss-free colloquium in which also Hevesy participated (see photo) further deepened the impression Bohr made on his colleagues in Germany. When the meetings were over Hevesy travelled northward together with Bohr and Aldebert Rubinowicz. He was so excited about the experience in Berlin that he wrote a long letter to Stefan Meyer: "I have never experienced an ovation similar to that given Bohr in Berlin. Young and old celebrated him with complete conviction and enthusiasm. He stayed with Planck, however for one day he was "claimed" by the younger generation; it was a boss-free conference, as Haber called it, in Dahlem with 18 participants who were then invited by Haber. In spite of a thousand questions put to him, Bohr arrived lively and joyful in Copenhagen.*

*1 May 1920 to Stefan Meyer*
"Niemals erlebte ich eine ähnliche Huldigung wie Bohr in Berlin dargebracht wurde, jung und alt feierte ihn mit voller Überzeugung und mit Begeisterung. Er wohnte bei Planck, wurde jedoch für einen Tag von der jüngeren Generation "in Anspruch genommen", es war ein Bonzenfreier Kongress wie ihn Haber taufte, in Dahlem mit 18 Teilnehmern, die dann bei Haber eingeladen waren. Trotzdem tausend an ihn gerichtete Fragen kam Bohr lebendig und fröhlich in Kopenhagen an".

The boss-free seminar in Berlin 1920, from left to right: Otto Stern, Wilhelm Lenz,
James Franck, Rudolf Ladenburg, Paul Knipping, Niels Bohr, E. Wagner, Otto v. Beyer,
Otto Hahn, G. v. Hevesy, Lise Meitner, Wilhelm Westphal, Hans Geiger, Gustav Hertz,
Peter Pringsheim, Courtesy: the Niels Bohr Archive.

The new institute building in Copenhagen which should have been
ready early in 1920 was not finished – as Bohr had indicated in his letters –
and Hevesy was offered temporary space at the institute of pathology.
This arrangement however never came to pass. When his first excitement
had subsided, he felt tired and indisposed; Bohr persuaded him to take a
long vacation in North Zealand, and Hevesy – unfit for idleness – used the
time to finish several articles and to work over some of the chapters of the
textbook on radioactivity. He had a lively correspondence with Paneth.
Not until the fall of that year did he resume experimental work together
with the Danish physico-chemist Johannes Brønsted. But soon he left for
Budapest, stopping on the way in Hamburg, so that he and Paneth could
bring their book into a publishable shape.

Bohr's new institute was finally opened in March 1921 and its scientific
staff consisted, beside Bohr and Hevesy, of the two Danish experimentalists Hans M. Hansen and Jacob C. Jacobsen. James Franck had come from
Germany to help organize the experimental section, and also the theoretical physicists Hans A. Kramers from Holland, Oscar Klein from Sweden,

and Svein Rosseland from Norway belonged to the group – all of them were co-workers and friends of Bohr's long before the institute was opened.

Although Hevesy was formally affiliated with the institute and Bohr had secured a stipend for him from the Rask Ørsted Foundation, he first worked with Brønsted at the Technical University on the separation of the mercury isotopes. They started by using a method that did not lead to satisfactory results, and therefore later changed their technique and made use of the difference in the rate of evaporation of the different isotopes, which was a much more efficient procedure. In the fall of 1920 Hevesy wrote Paneth that he had entered "die Sekte der Isotopentrenner" (the sect of the isotope separators).

In spite of his success in the laboratory and his enthusiasm for Denmark, the friendliness of her people, and the beautiful countryside, Hevesy felt at times depressed; from a convalescent home in North Zealand he wrote "I do my very best not to be depressed."\* His insomnia seriously affected his working capacity, and to Paneth he made the revealing remark (1 May 1921) "Unfortunately, it is the restlessness of my brain which keeps me from sleeping."\*\* This restlessness of his mind became worse as he grew older and caused him much discomfort. On the other hand, it is hard to imagine how he could have achieved all he actually did in these years, if he had been able to sleep at night and to relax when he was on vacation or travelling. Instead, he considered it his best "leisure" to read scientific journals and books. All through his life, he had an enormous appetite for acquiring additional knowledge within his own fields of interest. This is well illustrated by the fact that, about two decades later, he even ventured into the biological sciences. This ability to learn and to accumulate knowledge stayed with him over an unusually long period of time, well into his sixties. Aided by an excellent memory, he could easily avail himself of this immense body of useful information whenever he needed it.

\*25 May 1921 to Paneth
"ich tue mein möglichstes um nicht deprimiert zu sein."

\*\*1 May 1921 to Paneth
"Leider ist es die Unruhe in meinem Gehirn, die mich am Schlafen hindert".

The early 1920ies brought decisive advances in Bohr's theory, a development in which Hevesy took great interest although he did not contribute with new experimental results. The experimentalists at the institute centered on light spectroscopy while Hevesy's training and talents drew him to Brønsted's isotope separation work. One of the problems which occupied Bohr was to explain the periodic table of the elements developed by Mendelejev half a century earlier. Bohr suggested that the electrons around the atomic nucleus are arranged in shells and that only those electrons which are located in the outermost shell determine the chemical properties of any element. Since only a definite number of electrons is contained in each shell, a new one will be formed as the previous one is filled, and therefore similar chemical properties will be observed at regular intervals in the sequence from the lighter to the heavier elements. When Bohr put forward these ideas, not all the places in Mendelejev's periodic table were filled, some elements, among them the element which occupies place no 72 in the system, had not yet been discovered. All previous efforts to find and identify it by chemical means had failed, and Bohr indicated that this might be due to the fact that the chemists had assumed this element to be chemically similar to the rare earths. Bohr, however, expected the "missing element 72" to be a homologue to zirconium, and to belong to the titanium group.

At this point in the scientific development a variety of ideas and circumstances seemed to converge: for example, as mentioned before, eight years earlier Hevesy had been on his way to Oxford in order to learn X-ray spectroscopy from Moseley, but the outbreak of the First World War had prevented this collaboration. After Moseley's untimely death this technique had been further developed by among others Manne Siegbahn in Lund who, in 1921, was visited by Dirk Coster from Holland for a period of time. Together, they had built a new instrument which was much superior to the earlier models. Bohr thought that Coster might be able to introduce Siegbahn's technique at the Copenhagen institute and thus help to clarify the constitution of the rare earth elements; possibly even to identify the unknown element 72. On the invitation of Bohr, Coster came to Copenhagen in September 1922 in order to build an X-ray spectrograph.

1921 on the occasion of Haber's visit in Copenhagen. Standing: Niels Bohr, E. Güntelberg, I. Brøndsted. Seated: G. Hevesy, Mrs. A. Delbanco, Fritz Haber.
Courtesy: the Niels Bohr Archive.

During the summer of that same year Hevesy had become exceedingly interested in geochemistry, especially in the problems of the abundance of different elements and of the age of the earth. Also the rare earth elements, their chemical similarities, and their placement within the periodic system were topics of great actuality in this context.

Thus, the coincidence of Bohr's interest in the periodic law with Coster's arrival and the construction of the X-ray spectrograph, the arguments about the placement of the unknown element either among the rare earths or as a zirconium homologue, Hevesy's newly awakened interest in geochemistry – all these factors called for a new initiative that might give experimental evidence for or against Bohr's views.

Coster built the new instrument using parts that were purchased from Siegbahn, the rest was built and assembled at the institute's workshop. Hevesy took responsibility for the chemical work required to clarify this problem. It was clear that the proper materials in which one should look for element 72 were minerals rich in zirconium; the first sample material was provided by the geological institute of the university. It was also clear

51

that the amount of element 72 present in the mineral must be very small, and therefore it was necessary to remove as much as possible of the unwanted material through a chemical purification process.

The first X-ray spectrum of a purified sample gave some indication that the lines characteristic of element 72 were present. Therefore, the next step must be an attempt to separate the unknown element from zirconium. Hevesy went to work and – as he described it in his reminiscenses – was plain lucky in his choice of the method. He decided to dissolve as much of the sample as possible and to crystallize the double fluorides of zirconium. He found out much later that this was by far the best method of separating element 72 from the much larger quantities of zirconium present in the mineral. He ended up with a preparation which contained so much of the sought-after element that the X-ray spectrum of the sample very clearly showed the characteristic lines which had been calculated by Moseley on the basis of Bohr's assumptions.

This was a triumph for Hevesy and Coster who had overcome great experimental difficulties in order to prove that the unknown element 72 did not belong to the group of rare earths but was indeed similar to zirconium. It was also a triumph for Bohr whose theory about the constitution of the atoms and the periodic system had found another striking, experimental confirmation.

There was a good deal of both joyous and serious drama in the course of these events. While Hevesy and Coster's experiments were in progress, Bohr had been awarded the Nobel Prize – but when Bohr left for Stockholm in order actually to receive the prize, a definite proof that they had found element 72 in the zirconium rich mineral samples had not been obtained. As is customary, Bohr had to deliver his Nobel lecture before the Swedish Academy of Sciences the day after he had been presented with the award; the news that the latest experiments in Copenhagen were successful reached him in the evening through a phone call from Coster. Hevesy had jumped on the train to Stockholm in order to be present when Bohr would announce their finding – which he did towards the end of his talk. This caused great excitement in his audience, and the news spread fast all over Europe. In his frequent exchange of letters with Paneth during the early years in Copenhagen, Hevesy never mentioned the work on element 72. He wrote enthusiastically about Bohr's Nobel Prize and about his trip to Stockholm where he wanted to take part in the festivities. The first time he tells about the search for the unknown element is on 4 January 1923, and he begins the letter with the words "We have caught element 72"*. In his reply Paneth expressed genuine joy and admiration: he asked Hevesy to please cable permission to mention the discovery in a colloquium. Hevesy did not cable but he felt quite guilty about this and excused himself saying that he needed Coster's consent. In the months that followed he frequently asked his friend to send him chemicals and other material from Germany, which were not readily available in Denmark. Throughout the almost 46 years of their close friendship, Paneth's response to Hevesy's numerous demands remained the same: he was always ready to help.

Hevesy's and Coster's discovery gave rise to a serious and long-lasting drama, a frustrating experience for all involved: namely, the quarrel over the priority to this discovery between Hevesy and Coster on the one hand, and French and British scientists on the other. This priority conflict has been discussed and analyzed in detail recently by Kragh (ref. p. 122) and it will therefore be described here in outline, only. In addition to the original publications on this subject and the debates which appeared in scientific journals we may now base our evaluation on a report which Hevesy wrote in the summer of 1923. In this document he described the events as he saw them, but he decided at that time to withhold his report until the excitement had subsided and all scientists actively involved in the quarrel had passed away. In 1957 Hevesy sent these notes to Bohr, but they were not made available until about twenty years later. By that time, the dramatic conflict could be viewed objectively by the historians of science.

As mentioned before, it was assumed by most chemists that the unknown element 72 in the periodic table belonged to the group denoted as rare earths, which are chemically so similar that they are extremely difficult to separate from each other. In several European laboratories considerable efforts were made to prepare each element in a pure form.

*4 January 1923 to Paneth
"Wir haben Element 72 erwischt".

53

Since chemical separation seemed fruitless, it was an obvious step to try to identify these different elements on the basis of their light and X-ray spectra. Unfortunately, also these observations turned out to be ambiguous, which caused some scientists to look at the weak spectral lines on their photographic plates with a good deal of wishful thinking. It was tempting to "see" the lines and to interpret the spectra in accordance with one's expectations. Disbelieving Bohr's predictions, French chemists headed by Georges Urbain published their findings and stated that they had observed the spectral lines of the unknown element in a purified sample of the rare earths. They proposed that this newly discovered element should be named "Celtium". Urbain's observations could not be confirmed by other scientists who visited him and looked at the photographs of his spectra, but Urbain never stopped insisting that his results were correct. Also in England, the chemist Alexander Scott claimed that he had discovered the unknown element, but since his results could not be confirmed by others, he soon withdrew his claim. The name to be given to element 72 in the periodic table by Hevesy and Coster was also discussed in Copenhagen: some proposed that it be called "Danium" – but it was finally agreed to call it "Hafnium", derived from the Latin name of Copenhagen.

The controversy about the priority to the discovery of element 72 was also spiced by political and personal motives. The French felt hurt in their national pride when the results of Urbain and his associates were drawn in doubt. The British who proclaimed that Scott's results meant a victory for British science were more divided in their views. Rutherford had fully accepted Bohr's theory and was prepared to trust the Copenhagen results. Again, he had the role of the arbitrator and gave Hevesy and Coster his support. The British scientific journals however, were reluctant and Hevesy reports in a letter to Rutherford (11 January 1924) that although his paper about hafnium had been accepted in England, a referee remarked (confidentially reported to Hevesy by his friend Robert Lawson) that "we adhere to the original word celtium given to it by Urbain as a representative of the great French nation which was loyal to us throughout the war. We do not accept the word hafnium given to it by the Danes who only pocketed the spoils during the war" (incidentally, none of the discoverers were Danish citizens). This remark – although made by a scientist – should not be taken too seriously, nor should it be considered representative of the general attitude among British scientists. It may only serve to illustrate that political undertones were (are) to be found in scientific disputes at all times and in all countries, and they were not missing in the priority conflict about the discovery of element 72. One year later (29 February 1925) with a hint at the large number of papers which had already appeared, Rutherford wrote to Hevesy "I am glad to hear you are publishing the work on hafnium pretty widely. The name, I am sure, has come to stay".

Eventually, Hevesy and Coster did gain international recognition for their discovery. Between the fall of 1922 and 1925, Hevesy had published more than 30 papers and a book on hafnium. Five of these publications were written together with Coster, 8 with a Danish or Japanese co-author, and the rest under his own name alone. In January 1925, Hevesy complained in a letter to Paneth "I swim (am drowned) in French and English proofs. There is no end to this."* He did not only write papers, he travelled all over central Europe to lecture, and for the first time after the war he visited England and met Rutherford again. The wide interest in the discovery, its immediate confirmation of Bohr's theory, and the heated dispute over priority placed Hevesy (and Coster) in the center of interest of the scientific community. Early in 1924 (February 25) he wrote to his friend Stefan Meyer "In the beginning of April I travel to England on matters concerning hafnium and by the end of July to Bruxelles, where I am invited to the Solvay meeting. The Belgians are even more repudiating than the French, but with the invitation of Schrödinger and myself the first tentative approach has been made ... I am sorry that I come to Austria and Hungary on rarer and rarer occasions, but events push me steadily more towards the west. But I hope the time will come when I can spend a few enjoyable weeks in Vienna."** The first re-union with Rutherford after the war was an experience of great personal importance to Hevesy,

*21 January 1925 to Paneth
"ich schwimme in französischen und englischen Korrekturen – es nimmt kein Ende".
**25 February 1924 to Stefan Meyer
"Anfangs April fahre ich nach England in Hafnium Angelegenheiten und Ende Juli nach Brüssel, wo ich zum Solvay Kongress geladen bin. Die Belgier sind ja noch ablehnender als

whereas the invitation from Hendrik A. Lorentz, president of the scientific committee for the Solvay meetings, meant Hevesy's admission into the circle of prestigeous scientists.

Understandably Hevesy and Coster regarded themselves as suitable candidates for the Nobel Prize – and were viewed as such by many. When Coster visited Stockholm in the summer of 1923, the question was discussed rather openly among the scientists within and outside the circle of academy members who award the prize. It was no secret that Urbain had been a candidate for the chemistry award but had lost prestige after Hevesy and Coster presented such strong evidence against Urbain's claim of having discovered element 72. In fact, although the discovery of hafnium was recognized internationally within the next couple of years, this matter was deeply resented in some French circles for many, many years to come, and the Nobel committee therefore never could agree to honor Hevesy and Coster with the chemistry prize for the discovery of element 72.

Many years later Hevesy hinted at his disappointment with the Swedish Academy of Science when he explained that other honors, for example the Copley medal of the Royal Society in London, awarded him in 1949, meant much more than did the Nobel Prize which had been bestowed on so many ... in Hevesy's view not all equally deserving. Hevesy felt betrayed in his expectation, and his disappointment could not even be dispelled when he received the award 20 years later for the development of the tracer method.

In the mid 1920ies Hevesy carried out an extensive research program. The preparation and purification of hafnium present in minerals from different parts of the world was a difficult and time-consuming task. The atomic weight of hafnium was determined on more or less "pure" samples in a number of different laboratories, and the discrepancies which resulted caused some dispute until the method of purification had been perfected.

die Franzosen, doch ist mit Erwin Schrödinger und meiner Einladung die erste schüchterne Annäherung erfolgt. ... Es tut mir Leid, dass ich immer weniger und weniger nach Österreich und Ungarn komme, die Ereignisse drängen mich aber immer mehr nach dem Westen zu. Hoffentlich kommt aber die Zeit wo ich einige gemütliche Wochen wieder mal in Wien verbringen kann".

Moreover, Hevesy and especially Coster were interested in obtaining patents on the production of pure hafnium and the industrial application of this new material. Coster entered into negotiations with the Philips Company in Holland and Hevesy with the Auer Gesellschaft in Germany. The seeking of advice and consent from colleagues and experts, the drafting of contracts, as well as the discussion of economic problems required an extensive correspondence; but all these efforts did not lead to any substantial economic gain for Hevesy or Coster. Hafnium and its compounds turned out to be of relatively little interest to industry.

These activities brought Hevesy into contact with many scientists both in Europe and in the United States, colleagues with whom he had not collaborated earlier. Among them were two great personalities who came to play an important part in Hevesy's life, namely the Austrian chemist and industrialist Auer von Welsbach and the Swiss-born geochemist Victor M. Goldschmidt who in the 1920ies held a professorship in Oslo.

Auer had devoted a lifetime of research to the chemistry of the rare earth elements besides being the founder and director of the Auer Company, best known for its production of the "Auer lighters" which, for example, lit all gas powered street lights at the beginning of this century. In his private laboratory, Auer von Welsbach had attempted to prepare highly purified samples of all the elements of the rare earth group, and he generously supplied Hevesy with samples and with information. The friendly relationship with Auer lasted until Auer's death in 1929, and Hevesy used his collection of these precious samples again 5 years later in his studies of induced radioactivity which proved to be of great interest both in physics and chemistry.

V. M. Goldschmidt, an eminent mineralogist and geochemist, had been friendly with Hevesy already during their student years in Freiburg. The work with hafnium brought them together again, and Goldschmidt supplied Hevesy inter alia with samples of alvit from Norway, which turned out to contain considerably more hafnium than most other minerals that were analyzed. Since Hevesy had become so interested in geochemistry, especially in studies of the terrestrial abundance of elements, the contact with Goldschmidt resulted in a lively correspondence and a frequent exchange of information as well as of samples to be analyzed. Goldschmidt came to Copenhagen in order to familiarize himself with recent advances in X-ray spectroscopy, and Hevesy reciprocated by lecturing in Oslo when he was on his way to the Norwegian ski resorts which he visited repeatedly in these years. A few years later, during his Freiburg period, Hevesy resumed these studies. The close contact between Hevesy and Goldschmidt lasted for almost 25 years.

Hevesy's numerous publications and survey articles on different aspects of his work with hafnium bear witness to the great effort he invested in this project. In addition, his correspondence was extensive: he wrote to Paneth every few days to press for additional information or for the proofs of their book, explaining that it would be out-dated by the time it was to appear. In Hevesy's opinion – as expressed repeatedly also on later occasions – it was more important that a book be up-to-date rather than without errors or mistakes. Unaffected by Hevesy's impatience, Paneth proceeded at his own pace, meticulously editing every chapter. The first German edition of the "Lehrbuch der Radioaktivität" appeared in 1923, – by that time an improved English edition was in preparation. The translation of the book was in the hands of Robert Lawson of Sheffield, a physicist who had spent several years at the Radium Institute in Vienna and therefore was a personal friend of both Hevesy and Paneth. The translation took a much longer time than they had anticipated, and caused both of them a lot of work; proof reading and all the well known worries of authorship often drove Hevesy to despair.

It is hard to imagine how there could have been time and strength left for other activities. Nevertheless, the frail and sleepless Hevesy had not forgotten his favorite idea from the Manchester and Vienna time, namely to apply the indicator method which had been his main pre-occupation in previous years. Typically, he had established contacts with colleagues at different laboratories of Copenhagen University, the Veterinary and Agricultural University, the Technical University, the Radium Hospital, etc. He was always willing to give advice and to introduce the indicator method in fields other than analytical chemistry. For example, he had made experiments at the Agricultural University on the absorption and translocation of lead by plants; the results were published in 1923. But since the indicators available at that time were the salts of heavy metals and as such exceedingly toxic, they were not readily applicable to biological studies. Nevertheless, the following year – in spite of his pre-occupation with hafnium – Hevesy returned again to his indicator method in collaboration with the Danish dermatologist Svend Lomholt and the chemist Jens A. Christiansen. They studied the circulation of bismuth and lead in the animal organism using RaF, which is an isotope of bismuth, and RaD, which is an isotope of lead, as isotopic indicators. This investigation was instigated by the fact that bismuth was being used in the treatment of venereal disease although very little was known about its mode of action.

Hevesy worked hard, literally day and night; he concentrated on his research, his correspondence, and his papers, and he was not really interested in anything else. His colleagues began to comment on his bachelorship, and eventually in the fall of 1924 he followed the example set by several of the long-term visitors at Bohr's institute: he became engaged and soon married a very attractive Danish girl, Pia Riis. This marriage lasted till the end of his life.

As already mentioned, Hevesy was now famous; he received offers from German universities, but he was no longer in a hurry to leave the inspiring circle of friends at Bohr's institute and his laboratory facilities in Copenhagen. On the other hand, the chance of obtaining a permanent position in Denmark was small indeed and – as he had anticipated before he went to Copenhagen 5 years earlier – his future would probably lie at a German university. Inquiries came from Karlsruhe and Hannover as well as from Freiburg im Breisgau. He took his young wife on a trip to Germany and Hungary, and made several stops on the way to take another look at these cities and their universities. In Freiburg, he was greeted by some of his old friends and former teachers, and was again enchanted by the city's beautiful surroundings. But regrettably, the facilities offered him at the university were modest: the institute was old and poorly equipped, and few positions for assistants were available. His wife Pia liked the city and she did not mind settling there for some years. Hevesy returned to Copenhagen, he needed time to make up his mind, and also to negotiate the conditions offered him at different universities.

In the summer of 1925, Hevesy made a second trip to Freiburg, almost ready to accept the chair of physical chemistry, provided the university agreed to invest in the modernization of the institute and its equipment, and also to establish a number of positions for assistants. He also tried to find suitable living quarters for his family. When all these problems were solved to his satisfaction, he decided in favor of the move, however allowing himself nearly one more year in Copenhagen in order to conclude his work there. It seems that he made this decision with a heavy heart. In a letter to Paneth written in December 1925 he says:

"I have now made the difficult decision and have accepted Freiburg for the winter of 1926/27. Never has a decision been so hard on me. However, I am lacking the moral courage to stay here. A purely scientific and personal position is only attractive as long as one can produce something reasonable. I do not feel convinced that I shall be successful with this and therefore – with a heavy heart – I prefer a teaching post to my present one. There, the expectations one can have with regard to scientific achievements are rightly smaller. I can hardly find a position which is better than the one in Freiburg. Thus, with a heavy heart, I set out on my travel and move back to Freiburg, which I left in 1908."*

Paneth was not so impressed with Hevesy's heavy heart, he replied "Although your letter sounds more as if you were making a big sacrifice, I do not doubt, that you will enjoy Freiburg very much in the end".** Paneth was right: very soon Hevesy did consider Freiburg his second home after Budapest, although he was to move a few more times in the years to come.

*1 December 1925 to Paneth
"Ich habe nun mehr den schweren Entschluss gefasst und Freiburg für Winter 1926/27 angenommen. Niemals ist mir ein Entschluss so schwer gefallen. Es fehlt mir aber der moralische Mut hier zu bleiben. Eine reine wissenschaftliche und persönliche Stelle ist nur so lange schön zu bekleiden bis man was vernünftiges produzieren kann. Ich fühle mich nicht überzeugt, dass mir das gelingen wird und darum ziehe ich mit schwerem Herzen meiner jetzigen Stelle eine Unterrichtsstelle vor, wo die Ansprüche die man an die wissenschaftliche Leistung von einem stellt mit Recht geringer angemessen werden. Eine bessere Stellung als die in Freiburg kann ich schwerlich finden. So nehme ich also mit schwerem Herzen den Wanderstab in die Hand um wieder nach Freiburg zu ziehen, das ich in 1908 verliess."
**22 Dec. 1925 to Hevesy
"Wenn auch Dein Brief …. fast mehr so klingt als ob Du ein grosses Opfer auf Dich nehmen müsstest, zweifle ich doch nicht, dass es Dir in Freiburg schliesslich sehr gut gefallen wird."

G. Hevesy in Freiburg ca. 1928. Courtesy: the Hevesy family.

G. Hevesy and his wife Pia on vacation in Tisvilde (North Zealand). Courtesy: the Hevesy family.

It is easy to imagine that Hevesy felt exhausted after the intellectual and emotional excitement of the Copenhagen years. His working load and also the pace of his numerous activities was geared up beyond his physical strength. When the race was over the anti-climax was not far off. He suddenly felt old – although he was only 40 – and intellectually burnt out. Probably he did not truly believe that he already had reached the peak of his career, but he felt that he could not continue in the same hectic manner. The position as the head of an institute in Germany would allow him more freedom and fewer obligations to work in the laboratory; instead, he could direct others to carry out the experiments he considered of interest. On the other hand he would have to teach and lecture, something he had not tried before.

Undoubtedly, it was of the greatest importance that the position in Freiburg gave him economic security and allowed him to live comfortably, although without luxury, together with his family. His first child, Jenny was born before he moved to Freiburg. Hevesy's personal needs were

61

indeed modest: he did not smoke and rarely tasted a glass of wine. He never owned a car and had little interest in social activities or entertainment, but he loved nature: long walks or a trip to the Black Forest offered the best recreation from his constant intellectual activity. Every winter he went skiing either in Switzerland or in Norway, however in the company of other scientists so that he could talk shop in the evenings.

When Hevesy accepted the Freiburg professorship he definitely expected to settle down there for good and to make Freiburg his permanent home. A few years later (1929) he was offered a position in Frankfurt/M under exceedingly favorable conditions, but he turned the offer down mainly because he was tired of changing his surroundings and starting all over again. It was fortunate that he decided as he did because the stability he so longed for was not going to last regardless of where in Germany he had settled.

# Professorship in Freiburg
# im Breisgau 1927-1934

From the beginning, the Freiburg period brought Hevesy to what he may have imagined as his goal: a full professorship at one of the leading universities in Germany, an institute which was further enlarged a few years after he had taken over, a fair sized group of co-workers and students joined by visitors from abroad who came to work under Hevesy's leadership. He enjoyed the freedom which his established fame gave him. In fact he did not have to work nor to press on in order to add to his scientific reputation. He travelled extensively and was away from Freiburg for long periods. In 1929 he joined Rutherford and many other distinguished British scientists on a boat trip to South Africa where the British Association for the Advancement of Science held its annual meeting. In the party were also Aston, Eddington, Egerton, Fowler and others. On this trip Hevesy met the editor of Nature, Mr. Gregory, an acquaintance of some importance in the years to come. During the voyage, Rutherford and Hevesy received word that they would be awarded honorary degrees by the University of Cape Town. It pleased Hevesy tremendously that he was honored together with Rutherford, his great teacher and friend.

The following year he went to the United States where he held the George Fisher Baker Non-Resident Lectureship at Cornell – a post Paneth had filled before him. From there he proceeded on a trip around the world, which brought him to Japan. Co-workers from the Copenhagen years, first of all the Japanese physicist Yoshima Nishina, gave him an enthusiastic welcome. Nishina had spent seven and a half years in Europe and almost half that time at Bohr's institute where he participated both in purely theoretical work and in the hafnium project. Throughout the thirties, Hevesy corresponded often with Nishina and helped him for example to procure heavy water for the research he had started in Japan.

After the Second World War they re-established contact, but unfortunately did not meet again. Throughout his life, Hevesy remained in touch with most of his colleagues with whom he had common interests; he enjoyed the high esteem and warm friendship of many of his students and associates from all over the world.

Aside from his long journeys, Hevesy paid several shorter visits to England, Paris, Vienna, and his hometown Budapest. He went skiing in Switzerland every winter together with his distinguished British friends, and he repeatedly returned to Meran in the summer with his family – not to mention his frequent trips to scientific meetings and conferences. His wife accompanied him on most of these journeys, but his small children Jenny and George – the boy was born in 1928 – stayed with a trustworthy nurse and housekeeper; some of the reliable assistants from Hevesy's staff had to keep a watchful eye on them.

Scientifically, the Freiburg period was a relatively quiet one without the excitement or the outstanding achievements of the previous years – nor of those to come. The chemistry of hafnium and of the rare earth elements were further explored in close connection with a much more comprehensive study of the terrestrial and meteoritic abundance of these and chemically related elements. Hevesy and his co-workers perfected the method of X-ray analysis using fluorescent radiation, and he managed within the first years in Freiburg to acquire not only the necessary equipment but also to train a group of able and conscientious collaborators. Another subject was the search for radioactive elements, mainly among the rare earths. This work was made possible because Hevesy had a complete collection of these substances presented to him by Auer von Welsbach. However, he depended also on the generosity of his friend Hans Geiger who had invented and perfected a sensitive detector of weak beta radiation. The Geiger counter and the Wilson cloud chamber actually replaced the electroscope which had been used for almost three decades to measure the radiation emitted by radioactive substances. Hevesy observed that samarium is a radioactive element which emits alpha rays; this discovery aroused considerable interest because – as also Hevesy realized – in principle it could lead to the development of a new method for geological age determinations. At present, the age of minerals is being determined from the isotope ratios of the elements which are formed when radioactive uranium and thorium present in minerals decay into a series of radioactive daughter elements. Radioactive samarium, however, decays into a stable isotope of neodymium, another rare earth element. This isotope ratio can only be determined by mass spectrometry. To Hevesy's great disappointment, the accuracy of this method at that time was not sufficiently high. Not until the early 1980ies – long after Hevesy's death – mass spectrometers were perfected to such a degree that samarium-neodymium ratios could be measured accurately and thus became a powerful tool in terrestrial as well as planetary physics and chemistry. Hevesy also attempted to clarify the origin of the radiation emitted by naturally occurring potassium. To this end, he tried to separate the isotope K-39 from K-41 by distillation, hoping to find that the heavier fraction would emit an increased radiation. However, this expectation was not confirmed. Again – as in the case of samarium – the accurate measurement of very weak, low-energy radiation was difficult with the instrumentation available. Nor were the determinations of atomic weight, carried out in part by Otto Hönigschmid in München and later by Gregory Baxter in the United States, sufficiently accurate to solve this problem. A few years later, Hevesy arrived at the correct answer when he studied the induced radioactivity produced by neutron bombardment of potassium, scandium, and calcium. Then he was able to show that the natural radioactivity of potassium is due to the isotope K-40.

It is characteristic of Hevesy that he had a strong urge to present his ideas and the results of his work in a variety of contexts. He did that during the Vienna period and even more so while he worked with hafnium in Copenhagen. In Freiburg, he became an exceedingly prolific author: The publications from the first Freiburg years (1927-32), a total of about 60, half of which were co-authored by one of his many associates, show the diversity of subjects studied at his institute. Among these papers we find three in which Hevesy returned to the application of the indicator method to biological problems. They do not bring anything new because the situation was unchanged: the toxicity of the heavy metals which could serve as indicators seriously limited their use. A few years later (1932), Harold Urey discovered the heavy hydrogen isotope deuterium and soon presented Hevesy, his friend from the early Copenhagen years, with a sample of dilute heavy water. Hevesy did not hesitate a moment and used fish as well as his own body to study the turnover and total volume of water in the organism. However, during the Freiburg period these biological experiments did not play an important role in comparison with all the other projects pursued by his group.

During his visit in the United States Hevesy entered into negotiations with the Rockefeller Foundation which seemed willing to grant substantial support to his research and to the enlargement of his institute on the condition that the State of Baden (to whom the university in Freiburg belonged) would invest a matching amount. In his application to the Rockefeller Foundation, Hevesy mentioned as the main objectives of his research 1) the problem of nuclear stability approached from considerations of the abundance of the elements; 2) studies of diffusion and electrolytic conduction, and 3) studies concerning the radioactivity of potassium and rubidium. None of these topics, however, represent fundamentally new ideas. As an addendum, maybe of secondary importance, Hevesy mentioned biological studies – but deuterium had not yet been discovered when the application was submitted.

This very comprehensive program was accepted both by the Rockefeller Foundation and the ministry of the State of Baden and brought Hevesy even closer to ideal working conditions in Freiburg. He was indeed well on his way to settle down for good and to enjoy his fame and stable position. He was leading a comfortable bourgeois life, keeping up his international contacts, and supervising his co-workers and students. Before his return from the trip around the world, his mother had died in Budapest and he thought that this meant the end of his earlier, very strong attachment to Hungary. In a letter to Stefan Meyer of 20 May 1931 he calls this "an almost complete break with the past" and continues" "if, until now, Freiburg was 75% my home, it will from now on be 100%."* Apparently, the political development in Germany, foreboding drastic changes of this situation, did not disturb him. He undertook steps to bring Rutherford to

*20 May 1931 to Stefan Meyer
"einen nahe vollständigen Bruch mit der Vergangenheit. .... Wenn Freiburg bisher zu etwa 75% meine Heimat war, wird es nun mehr bis zu 100% sein".

Freiburg, not only for a lecture but primarily to receive an honorary degree. Rutherford, however was concerned about the political trend in Germany; he hesitated, and a few months later flatly refused to accept any honors in Nazi Germany.

In the spring of 1933 Hevesy fell ill with whooping cough, was miserable and unable to work. It really shocked him when he received a letter from Paneth who, a few years earlier, had moved to Königsberg as a full professor of chemistry. Paneth explained that he was "on leave" (because of his Jewish descent) and trying to find a job in England where he intended to stay even if this meant a very modest standard of living and a subordinate position at any British university. In Hevesy's circle of friends and colleagues, the next to be dismissed were Fajans and V. M. Goldschmidt and it began to dawn on him that Freiburg after all might not be his "permanent home". On July 5, he wrote Paneth "I am about to conclude my work as far as possible. The III Reich is something very beautiful for a German, but if one is not a German it seems to me the most correct (best) to draw the conclusions, regardless how unpleasant they may be in my case."* It is surprising that he found the Third Reich "something wonderful for Germans" and even more so that he gave his nationality "not being a German" as a reason for the "unpleasant consequences", namely to give up his position at the university.

Apparently, it had taken Hevesy a few months to realize that the Nazi rulers meant what they said. He had never mentioned his "racial background" – in the Hitlerian sense of this term – but always presented himself as the Hungarian aristocrat with close links to the Magyar nobles. As a natural result of his upbringing and the traditions of the wealthy and assimilated jewry in Hungary, his political orientation was conservative. It found its German counterpart in the nationalist party (die Deutsch-Nationale Partei). In these circles, Hevesy would have been accepted readily and without further questioning in the early thirties. But this

*5 July 1933 to Paneth
"Ich bin dabei meine Arbeiten so weit als möglich abzuschliessen. Das III. Reich ist was sehr schönes für einen Deutschen, wenn man aber kein Deutscher ist, so scheint es mir am richtigsten zu sein, die Konsequenzen zu ziehen, wie unangenehm sie auch in meinem Punkte sein mögen".

section within the political spectrum – which in fact brought Hitler to power – was soon overrun; their ideas may have been on Hevesy's mind when he wrote that the Third Reich was something wonderful for Germans. It must have been quite clear to him that he could not possibly document his "Aryan" descent, as would be required by the authorities if he were to remain a full professor at a German university. In his letter to Paneth of 5 July 1933, he continues "In the beginning of August I shall travel to Denmark for a visit of about a fortnight, later to my fatherland: My later plans are still in the dark".* As mentioned on the preceding page, two years earlier Hevesy had written to Stefan Meyer that, after the death of his mother, he felt Freiburg was 100% his home; he had almost completely severed himself from the past. When he realized that Nazi Germany could not be his home after all, he re-discovered his bonds to the country where he was born and traveled to his "Heimat", his fatherland Hungary. His letter to Paneth of August 8 tells of his decision to return to Copenhagen, where he felt that he really belonged. It is understandable that Hevesy's emotions and attachments shifted back and forth: he was indeed homeless and he did not become rooted anywhere throughout his long adult life.

While he was vacationing in Denmark in August of 1933 together with his wife and his three children – his son George and his second daughter Ingrid were born in Freiburg – he informed Paneth confidentially (8 August 1933) "The decision to ask for my dismissal is not an easy one; for me the most agreeable solution would therefore be if the government dismissed me spontaneously. In this case I should in no way have to reproach myself in the future for having acted overhastily. I have therefore not done the least to make the decision of the government more difficult. Should my dismissal not come forward within the next few months I shall ask for it myself. I intend to move to Copenhagen where I shall find good working conditions, whether financial support will be possible has not yet been cleared up but hopefully also in this regard something will be found. I concluded from Rutherford's letter and the utterances of Donnan that they

*"Ich werde anfangs August für einen Besuch von etwa 14 Tagen nach Dänemark, später in meine Heimat (sic.) fahren: Meine späteren Pläne schweben im Dunkeln".

are willing to give me an opportunity for work in England, and emigration to England has some advantages. In the case of a European conflagration one is much further away from being involved in England as compared to Denmark. A consideration which applies not to myself but to my children. Also conditions in England are on a much grander scale than in Denmark, the possibilities much greater. On the other hand, I am already rooted in this country, also my wife is from Denmark and therefore my children have a national right to live here. Because national exclusiveness will probably grow strongly in all countries. The struggle for life and the political orientation inexorably lead in this direction. I ask you to treat the above information as confidential."*

In fact Rutherford did offer his assistance: He was actively supporting many efforts in Britain to help and to find positions for the German scientists who had been or were expected to be dismissed. In a letter of 12 May 1933 he invited Hevesy to Cambridge, however without specifying the conditions he might be able to offer. Hevesy did consider this possibility in the light of the threatening "European conflagration" (cf. letter of 8 August 1933) but this political viewpoint was outweighed by the

*8 August 1933 to Paneth
"Der Entschluss, um meine Entlassung einzureichen, fällt mir nicht leicht, die angenehmste Lösung für mich wäre deshalb, wenn mich die Regierung spontan entlassen würde. In diesem Falle könnte ich mir in der Zukunft den Vorwurf eines voreiligen Handelns unter keinen Umständen machen. Ich habe deshalb auch nicht das geringste unternommen die Entschliessung der Regierung zu erschweren. Sollte in den nächsten Monaten meine Entlassung nicht erfolgen so werde ich um sie selber ansuchen. Ich habe vor nach Kopenhagen zu ziehen, wo ich gute Arbeitsgelegenheiten finden werde; ob eine finanzielle Hilfe möglich sein wird, ist noch nicht geklärt aber hoffentlich wird sich auch in dieser Hinsicht etwas ergeben. Ich entnahm Rutherford's Schreiben sowie Donnan's Ausserungen, dass sie gewillt sind mir in England eine Arbeitsmöglichkeit zu geben und die Übersiedelung nach England hätte manches für sich. Im Falle einer europäischen Konflagration ist man in England viel weiter als in Dänemark davon entfernt herangezogen zu werden. Eine Überlegung die nicht für mich sondern für meine Kinder gilt. Auch sind die Verhältnisse in England viel grossartiger als in Dänemark, die Möglichkeiten viel grösser. Demgegenüber steht dass ich in diesem Lande bereits Wurzel gefasst habe, ferner dass meine Frau aus Dänemark stammt, meine Kinder demnach eine nationale Existenzberechtigung haben. Denn die nationale Exklusivität wird in allen Ländern vermutlich stark zu nehmen. Der Kampf ums Dasein und die politischen Richtlinien führen unerbittlich in diese Richtung. – – –
Ich bitte Dich die obigen Mitteilungen als vertraulich zu betrachten."

69

feeling that he had roots in Denmark and that his wife and children had their national origin there, which he found a strong argument in favor of Copenhagen. However, only a couple of years later Hevesy had doubts about whether this decision had been the right one.

Was an earlier chapter in Hevesy's life story about to repeat itself? After the First World War and during the revolution in Hungary he had found himself squeezed between political forces – first from the left and later from the right – which were threatening his personal freedom, jeopardizing his academic career, even blackmailing him personally. He realized that he had no future in his native country and decided to emigrate. As described in the preceding chapter, Bohr not only provided hospitality and economic support, but first of all the scientific and intellectual inspiration that led to Hevesy's impressive achievements in Copenhagen in the twenties. The crisis that threatened Hevesy 13 years later was different in many respects and so was his reaction to it. However, the results he was going to achieve this time were even more spectacular. Hevesy's tactical moves vis-à-vis Freiburg university were almost the opposite to his action in 1919 in Budapest: Now, he wanted to be dismissed rather than ask for his dismissal. The reason behind this attitude is not obvious. It would not have made any difference with regard to his chances to be offered a position outside Germany whether he was dismissed – as hundreds of others – or he had left Nazi Germany on his own initiative, as many did. Maybe, he did not expect the political development in Germany to be quite as violent and irreversible as it turned out to be, and he wanted to keep the door open in case German universities were to return to normal and stable conditions.

When Hevesy's decision to leave became known in the Freiburg university circles, it was deeply resented and deplored. His personality, his friendliness, his extremely polite and elegant manners together with his reputation as an outstanding scientist and an inspiring teacher made him exceedingly popular not only among his students and colleagues but also among subordinates and people from different walks of life. No wonder that everybody tried hard to make him stay in Freiburg. Many of his colleagues did not foresee what was in store for them and did not realize that the impression Hevesy gave of himself, although natural to him, did not represent all facets of his identity. Throughout his youth and adolescence he had belonged to the catholic Magyar nobility, and until Hitler decreed new definitions of ethnic terms, there was no conflict on Hevesy's mind. The introduction of racial laws in Germany, however did give rise to a serious conflict – as it did for innumerable others who had considered their "racial" background a matter of little or no concern and felt like equal citizens of their country. For the second time in his life, Hevesy was made homeless and uprooted – this time not in consequence of the overthrow of an old social order, as was the case in Hungary 13 years earlier, but primarily because his ancestors belonged to a minority group which – according to Hitler – no longer was permitted to be assimilated into the society of which they were a part.

It is remarkable that Hevesy – at least in his conversations and his letters to friends and acquaintances – could express optimism and see the positive rather than the negative aspects of his new situation. When he realized that everything he so successfully had built up in Freiburg was about to collapse, he accepted Bohr's offer with great anticipation and did not worry too much about the uncertainties which again burdened his future in Denmark. Quite to the contrary, he convinced himself that Denmark was the place where he really belonged, and he made himself believe that the losses he suffered by leaving Freiburg were more than compensated for by the gains of being reunited with Bohr.

Hevesy wrote to Paneth on 25 August 1933.

"... We left Hornbæk on the 17th, stayed for 4 days with the Bohrs in their princely mansion and are now in Hungary. I found Bohr grander and greater than ever. Most people do not grow any more when they have reached the age of 40. His fantastic personality develops more and more. I left with the impression that even without the unpleasant development in Germany, my place is really in Copenhagen and if one has the chance to live in the environment of such a unique person, one should not live somewhere else. I have already completely overcome leaving my institute in Freiburg. What I have not yet overcome is saying goodbye to my colleagues and students with whom I had a cordial relationship. For example, I saw Staudinger almost every day and we always discussed all the details of our teaching and carried them out together. By the way, I

71

shall spend the winter in Freiburg and thereafter do the moving. Financially, I shall be considerably worse off in Copenhagen than you are, but I have never been guided in my decisions by financial considerations. If necessary, one has to curtail further, which is definitely possible, although not agreeable. I have been very happy in Freiburg and I do not feel less happy about coming to Copenhagen. What more can one ask for. I am in Hungary until the beginning of October and then in Freiburg where I shall spend the winter.

As regards my moving to Copenhagen, I ask you for the time being to treat this confidentially. I consider it to be more correct if my colleagues learn this from me rather than indirectly. I am letting the government of Baden take precedence, if they do not dismiss me I shall ask for my dismissal by the end of October.
Many cordial regards from house to house ..."*

---

*25 August 1933 to Paneth
"... Wir verliessen Hornbæk den 17ten, wohnten vier Tage lang bei Bohr in seinem fürstlichen Hause und sind nun in Ungarn. Ich fand Bohr grossartiger und grösser als je. Die meisten Menschen wachsen nicht mehr wenn sie die Vierziger erreicht haben. Seine fabelhafte Persönlichkeit entwickelt sich immer weiter und weiter. Ich schied mit dem Eindruck dass sogar ohne der unerfreulichen Entwicklung in Deutschland mein Platz eigentlich in Kopenhagen ist und dass wenn man in der Umgebung eines so einzigartigen Menschen leben kann, man nicht anderswo leben soll. Mein Freiburger Institut zu verlassen habe ich bereits ganz verschmerzt, was ich noch nicht verschmerzt habe ist das Scheiden von meinen Kollegen und Studenten mit denen ich im herzlichsten Verhältnis stehe. Staudinger sah ich z.B. fast jeden Tag und wir haben alle Einzelheiten des Unterrichts stets besprochen und gemeinsam durchgeführt. Ich werde den Winter übrigens noch in Freiburg verbringen und dann erst die Übersiedelung vornehmen. Finanziell werde ich in Kopenhagen beträchtlich schlechter stehen als Du, doch liess ich mich niemals in meinen Entscheidungen durch finanzielle Erwägungen leiten. Man muss sich eben gegebenenfalls weiter einschränken, das durchaus möglich, wenn auch nicht angenehm ist. Ich war sehr glücklich in Freiburg und fühle mich nicht weniger glücklich nach Kopenhagen zu kommen. Was kann man sich mehr wünschen.
Ich bin bis anfangs Oktober in Ungarn (address) und dann in Freiburg wo ich den Winter noch verbringen werde.- - -
Was meine Übersiedelung nach Kopenhagen betrifft so bitte ich die vorerst als vertraulich zu betrachten. Ich halte es richtiger, dass meine Kollegen es von mir und nicht auf Umwegen erfahren. Den Vortritt habe ich der badischen Regierung gegeben, wenn sie mich nicht entlässt, so werde ich Ende Oktober für meine Entlassung einkommen.
Viele herzliche Grüsse von Haus zu Haus sendet Dein Georg."

72

Mein lieber F᎗᎗! Es hat mich
ausserordentlich gefreut von Dir zu
hören. Dein Schreiben wurde mir
hieher nachgesandt. Wir ver-
liessen Kornbach den 17ten. wohnten vier Tage lang
bei Bohr in seinem köstlichen Hause und sind nun
in Ungarn. Ich fand Bohr grossartiger und grösser
als je. Die meisten Menschen wachsen nicht mehr wenn
sie die Vierziger erreicht haben. Seine fabelhafte Persönlichkeit entwickelt sich immer weiter und weiter.
Ich schied mit dem Eindruck, dass sogar ohne der unerfreulichen Entwicklung in Deutschland mein Platz
eigentlich in Kopenhagen ist und dass wenn man
in der Umgebung eines so einzigartigen Menschen
leben kann, man nicht anderswohin soll. Mein
Freiburger Institut zu verlassen habe ich bereits ganz
verschmerzt. Was ich noch nicht verschmerzt habe
ist das Scheiden von meinen Kollegen und Studenten
mit denen ich im herzlichsten Verhältnis stehe.
Skrudinger sehe ich z. B. fast jeden Tag und wir
haben alle Einzelheiten des Unterrichts stets besprochen
und gemeinsam durchgeführt. Ich werde den

TÁPIÓ-SÁP
PEST-MEGYE
TEL. TÁPIÓ-SÁP 6.

1933 25 VIII

Winter übrigens noch in Freiburg verbringen und dann erst d
Übersiedelung vornehmen. Finanziell werde ich in Kop.
schließlich schlechter stehen als du, doch lasse ich mich
niemals in meinen Entscheidungen durch finanzielle
Erwägungen leiten. Man muss sich eben gegebenenfalls
weiter einschränken, das durchaus möglich, wenn
auch nicht angenehm ist. Ich war sehr glücklich in
Freiburg und hielt mich nicht weniger glücklich nach
Kopenhagen zu kommen. Was kann man sich mehr
wünschen!

It is astounding that Hevesy, at the age of 49 and with a family of four, his wife and three children, was able to readjust so fast to a complete reshaping of his existence.

After his vacation in Denmark and in Hungary during the summer of 1933, he decided to return to Freiburg for another year in order to bring his own work and that of his graduate students to some kind of a conclusion. He was still waiting for the government of Baden to dismiss him. It seemed important to him to establish that his departure from Freiburg was not caused by a decision he had wanted to make, but was forced upon him by the Nazi regime. In fact, Hevesy stayed on at the University of Freiburg for a whole year – until August 1934 – without letting his colleagues know that he had made the decision to leave. He informed the Rockefeller Foundation of his plans and had to accept that the funds granted for his work in Freiburg could not be transferred to Copenhagen. Finally, in July 1934, he asked for his dismissal and his request was met on 25 August 1934.

*Second Copenhagen Period 1935-1943:*
# The Development of the Tracer Method

During the span of time Hevesy was a professor of physical chemistry in Freiburg, nuclear physics had progressed at an enormous pace. Frédéric and Irène Joliot-Curie in Paris had observed that bombardment of aluminum with alpha particles led to the formation of an unstable, that is to say radioactive element which – within a short time – disintegrated and returned to a stable state. James Chadwick in England had found a new elementary particle, the neutron, which carries no charge but a mass equal to that of the proton. Shortly thereafter, Enrico Fermi and his co-workers in Rome used this new particle to bombard a number of light elements and they observed that one or more unstable, radioactive isotopes were formed in each case. It soon became clear that almost any stable element in the periodic table – when bombarded with neutrons – was transformed into at least one radioactive isotope which was chemically different from the bombarded one. In many cases, for example that of radio-phosphorus, the radioactive nuclei formed emitted an electron and were transformed back into the element of the original target. The rate at which this spontaneous re-transformation occurred varied from element to element, ranging from fractions of a second to thousands or even millions of years.

Hevesy had always regretted that the radioactive elements he had used in his chemical indicator experiments were so toxic that they could not be applied in biological studies. Shortly before he left Freiburg, he had taken up heavy hydrogen as an indicator, but in view of Fermi's results, the situation improved dramatically. Artificially produced radioactive elements were to bring Hevesy world renown, he became an innovator, especially in the life sciences.

For a relatively long period before the 1930ies, there was no direct interaction between science and the political situation in Western Europe.

With the fateful rise of the Nazi regime in Germany, a situation of this kind suddenly existed. The coincidence of a number of factors, some of them scientific, others political or economic, strongly affected the course of events for several decades to come. These factors played an important role also at Niels Bohr's institute in Copenhagen where Hevesy resumed experimental work early in 1935.

The author of the present account entered the scientific scene at the start of this period. As a newly hatched Ph.D. in physics and a Jewish refugee from Germany, I was accepted at the institute in Copenhagen in the spring of 1934, and was asked to assist Professor James Franck who arrived in Copenhagen almost at the same time. He had resigned from his position in Göttingen. Although Franck was a close friend of Bohr's and had stayed at the institute on several occasions since its foundation in 1921, his visit was not expected to be of very long duration. Negotiations with American universities were in progress, and early in 1935 Franck accepted a chair at the Johns Hopkins University in Baltimore. His departure in the summer of that year was deplored by all his friends and colleagues in Denmark.

Several months before Franck left for the United States, Bohr suggested that I continue my work at the institute as an assistant to Hevesy who was expected to arrive from Freiburg in the late fall. I recall how Bohr explained to me that the exciting new results with artificially produced radioactive isotopes undoubtedly would capture my interest, and that both he and Hevesy were eager to take up this new field. Since the institute was equipped mainly for spectroscopy, it was imperative at this point to concentrate on the building of instruments for radioactivity measurements. This was a field I knew very little about but Otto Robert Frisch, who presently worked in England, was due to come to the institute, and maybe – said Bohr – he could teach me how to build these instruments, so we could follow up and carry on Fermi's research.

Thus, although my work with Franck continued while Hevesy moved into his new apartment and re-established himself in the familiar Copenhagen surroundings – in between travelling to various places – Frisch and I began to build Geiger counters and simple amplifiers; we used the telephone company's call counter to register the number of beta particles that passed the counter for example from a small sample of a uranium salt.

Hevesy started his work in the early spring using the precious rare earth preparations he had obtained from Auer von Welshbach. It was revealing to discover recently that Fermi had written to Hevesy in October 1934 asking him for small quantities of these elements for experiments with neutrons; but Hevesy gave a rather evasive answer, referring him to other people who might have some of this material. As his first project he intended to investigate the induced radioactivity of the rare earths and a few other elements which he had studied earlier, such as hafnium, scandium, and potassium.

His approach to the field proved to be most successful and important; first: the induced radioactivity and the radiation properties of these elements were established and described. Second: on the basis of his observations, Hevesy could prove that the potassium isotope K-40 is responsible for the natural radioactivity of potassium – a problem he had tried to solve earlier without arriving at an unambiguous result. Third: the most important discovery from this short period of research was the basic development of neutron activation analysis.

As discussed in the previous chapter, the separation and purification of the different elements within the group of rare earths was exceedingly complex. Chemists in many countries were still laboring with this problem using the classical methods of analytical chemistry. Hevesy suggested that – as a means of identification – we make use of the characteristic decay period of each of these elements and of their relative intensities of activation after neutron bombardment. In this way, their presence could be determined in any unknown mixture. In the early phase of this work we observed that, with the neutron sources available, the strongest activity was induced in the rare earth element dysprosium. It was therefore easy to detect even a minute amount of a dysprosium compound present as an impurity in the salt of any other rare earth element. This finding was published in 1936. The classical test object Hevesy used one year later was a sample of gadolinium which Luigi Rolla of Florence had tried to purify from traces of europium. We could see from the decay of the induced radioactivity that the sample consisted of two components decaying at different rates. Hevesy then added varying quantities of "impurity" to the purified gadolinium, and we compared the resulting changes in intensity of radiation from the two components. It was possible with this technique not only to identify the impurity but also to estimate how much of it was present. As we look back on these pioneer experiments today we must keep in mind that the neutron sources available at that time – the well-known mixture of radon gas with beryllium powder enclosed in glas ampullas – were very weak ones, and so was the resulting radioactivity of the bombarded sample. Fifty years later, a nuclear reactor is used as the neutron source; it is at least ten million times stronger than Hevesy's sources. Therefore, the sensitivity of this method of analysis is now correspondingly higher. The term "neutron activation analysis" was coined in the fifties when the method was adapted to the powerful neutron source and was made much more sophisticated by means of electronic analyzers. Today the technique has wide application in radiochemistry, technology and studies of environmental contamination.

While the exciting work with artificially produced radio-isotopes of the rare earths was in progress, Hevesy became more and more interested in the production of a radio-isotope of one of the lighter and biologically interesting elements. Radio-phosphorus seemed to be the obvious candidate. Its production and properties had been described by Fermi whose results were confirmed at the Bohr Institute. Radio-phosphorus can be produced by bombarding sulphur with neutrons; it decays under emission of a fairly penetrating beta radiation (electrons) and its rate of decay (half-life) is about 14 days. These are most attractive properties. The half-life is conveniently long so that biological experiments on animals or plants can be performed; the electrons are easy to detect by means of a Geiger counter, and the element phosphorus plays an important part in living organisms, f.ex. as calcium phosphate in the skeleton or as inorganic and organic phosphorus compounds for example nucleic acid and the energy transfer molecule ATP present in practically all tissue.

Thus, Hevesy set out to produce radio-phosphorus so that he could feed or inject radioactive sodium phosphate into animals and find out what happened. Today the description of his procedure and of the home-made instruments used to measure the distribution and excretion of the phosphorus injected, impresses us as rather primitive; at the same time we marvel that Hevesy could arrive at such epoch-making results.

In retrospect it is equally impressive that the concept of "radioactive indicators", first conceived and applied in Manchester and Vienna before the First World War as a tool in analytical chemistry, grew far beyond its original use into much wider, more complex and less tangible domains. When Hevesy ventured into this entirely new field, he had not designed his experiments with any clear expectation of what he might observe. However, he must have discussed his plans with Ole Chievitz, the head surgeon of the Finsen Hospital, a classmate and close friend of Bohr's and also a friend of Hevesy. Chievitz placed the experimental animals, laboratory facilities, and even a technician at Hevesy's disposal, so that all practical problems were taken care of. After the animals had been injected, samples were taken, and brought into a manageable form by combustion or by being dissolved in acid followed by precipitation of phosphate.

They were then brought to the institute where the Geiger counters were located and all radioactivity measurements were carried out for many years to come.

The first publication dealing with the new application of radioactive indicators described the pioneer experiment with P-32 injected into rats. This report had the form of a letter to the editor of *Nature*. It was submitted in September 1935 and signed by both Hevesy and Chievitz. The authors not only described the experiment and presented the results, they – that is to say Hevesy – made a rather sweeping statement of interpretation which was not in agreement with the views widely held at that time. It reads: "The results strongly support the view that the formation of the bones is a dynamic process, the bones continuously taking up phosphorus atoms which are partly or wholly lost again and are replaced by other phosphorus atoms". The editor of *Nature*, an anonymous ruler over what was accepted and what was rejected by this most prestigeous of science journals, was Mr. Gregory with whom Hevesy had travelled to South Africa in 1929. He accepted this remarkable paper but took some precaution in an editorial comment printed a few pages further on, where he laconically noted "The authors further believe that the formation of the bone is a dynamic process, involving continuous loss and replacement". It seems that he wanted to place himself at some distance from such untraditional thinking.

This pioneer experiment was a signal to the biologists: while Hevesy's earlier application of the indicator method was of interest mainly to analytical chemistry, it was now the biologists' turn to learn what isotopic indicators are all about. The basic fact is this: artificially produced radioactive phosphorus atoms are chemically identical with the naturally occurring, stable phosphorus atoms, and therefore they follow the stable phosphorus atoms in metabolic processes. However, they can be observed because as they decay they emit electrons which give rise to a pulse in a Geiger counter. In other words, the use of radioactive indicators enables us to distinguish between atoms which entered any given organism at the time of the experiment from those (of the same element) which had been there before. Consequently, the location and the movement of these "labelled" atoms or molecules as a function of time, their exchange with stable ones present in the system, and their incorporation into different compounds can be observed. This means that processes which up to the present were unobservable in principle can now be studied. Naturally, the method lends itself especially to the investigation of dynamic processes.

In the course of the next few years Hevesy sometimes placed his observations in a most untraditional context. It was not his style to plan and let his co-workers perform laborious experiments which had to be repeated several times; nor would he plough through the literature looking for supporting or contradicting evidence, nor make elaborate calculations. Quite to the contrary: he performed only very few experiments, launched into an interpretation of the results, and – since writing presented no difficulty for him – put it all on paper immediately. He sent off the manuscript for publication within a short time. I even remember situations where Hevesy had the manuscript ready before the experiments were concluded. He impatiently asked for the last results and inserted the figures in the text. He was convinced that the experimental results would confirm his expectation.

Hevesy had a flair for choosing the problems which could be clarified by means of the indicator method, for example the interrelation between the components of a complicated system, and in the large majority of cases, his intuition brought him on the right track in spite of the fact that – when he began this work – his knowledge in the fields of biology and biochemistry

81

was scanty, to say the least. Thus, about half a year after his arrival in Copenhagen, Hevesy had introduced a new technique into the life sciences, which he had been dreaming of for almost 20 years.

I have already given a brief outline of the development in nuclear physics, which made the application of the indicator method possible, and also of Hevesy's departure from Freiburg and the consequences of his move. In Copenhagen, Hevesy had very modest laboratory facilities, no economic backing, just one young assistant. But in his opinion – already quoted in the preceding chapter – he had truly gained because he valued the re-union with Bohr and with the Copenhagen institute so highly. I vividly remember an episode which took place in the spring of 1935: James Franck and Hevesy met in the laboratory and Franck made a nostalgic remark about the "old days in Göttingen" which he missed painfully. Hevesy responded in an almost merry and at the same time encouraging tone: "Herr Kollege", he explained, "I am happy to be rid of all these troubles of running an institute. No more administrative duties, no more worries about raising funds, and, first of all, no more problems with co-workers, their future careers and their personal conflicts. I feel so relieved" – said Hevesy. Franck shook his head sadly; it was not his approach. He was lonesome for his co-workers whose sorrow and happiness he had shared. A greater contrast in outlooks of two great personalities can hardly be imagined.

At this point it may be appropriate to describe the general impression Hevesy made on his young assistant during the first years of our collaboration. Hevesy was tall and slender, his head and face were long and oval. As he moved about meeting people in the building, he had a friendly somewhat ironic and sometimes mocking smile on his lips. He was exceedingly polite and always addressed his subordinates in the same friendly manner as his colleagues and personal friends. He used to be dressed in an elegant, somewhat old-fashioned style; his cut-away or other tailored suits, for example, had been down-graded to everyday use. In bad weather he wore galoshes so that the presence of one – or sometimes two – of these boots outside his office door was a signal to us that he had either come or gone. Hevesy had the perfect manners of the Austrio-Hungarian aristocracy, which were noticeably different from those of the Scandinavian educated middle class, the background of most of his colleagues. Thus, my first impression of the new boss was that of an affable, remarkably polite gentleman, very conventional in his behaviour and impersonal in his relation with people. I felt there would probably never develop the kind of close personal contact – and friendship – that had made my relationship with James Franck such a unique experience.

When Hevesy entered the laboratory, his first remark inevitably was "good day, good day – are you fine, – yes." As the concluding "yes" indicated, he took it for granted that the person so addressed was feeling fine. It did happen – although rarely – that my answer was "no". This caused a complete derailment of his thoughts and forced him to ask what was wrong rather than to proceed to whatever scientific topic he had meant to talk about.

Hevesy spoke many languages with ease, including Danish, of course, and all of them with the typical Hungarian accent; he often mixed them freely – both in speaking and in writing – using whichever term first came to his mind. Although, for periods of several years, Hevesy had lived in an English, a German, and a Danish speaking country, aside from his native Hungary, he did not master any of the languages correctly, as is apparent from the numerous verbal quotations I have used to document his views. I soon found out that Hevesy was not a dexterous experimentor. He often hurt himself and became a well-known figure at the nearby emergency ward of the Rigshospital. When he did hurt himself badly, his reaction was that of a stoic. One of the episodes I remember clearly occured when Hevesy had burnt his arm with hot concentrated sulphuric acid. He came back from the hospital with his arm thoroughly bandaged, his face was rather pale. His secretary suggested that he go home and take a rest, but his laconic reply was: "Do you think it hurts less when I go home?" Instead, he disappeared into his office and closed the door.

Regardless of several minor accidents, Hevesy loved to fiddle with the instruments or with chemical procedures. When he found himself alone in the laboratory for a few moments, he would invariably take some readings of the counters and splash the notebooks with ink from his malfunctioning fountain pen; he would alter the voltage over the counter in any arbitrary direction, or change the sample that was being measured – as a rule to the

Niels Bohr, James Franck, George Hevesy at the Copenhagen institute 1935.
Courtesy: The Niels Bohr Archive.

despair of whoever was in charge of the measurements. Many years later, while reading his autobiographical notes and his letters from the early years of his career in which he described his classical experiments, I often wondered whether, as a younger man, he was in better control of his manual skills. However, I have never seen him angry or reproachful when something went wrong in the laboratory, regardless of who was at fault.

From the very beginning of our collaboration, Hevesy's personality made a great impression on me. He was not the gentle, loving, solicitous father figure that was James Franck; he was not the shy and at the same time overwhelmingly impressive Niels Bohr whose radiant personality pervaded the whole atmosphere at the institute. Hevesy was the dynamic promoter of new adventures, he was inspiring, his enthusiasm was contagious and demanding – as many of his "victims" will confirm with some misgivings. He expected his co-workers to make serious efforts and to work hard, and he got what he wanted by way of his friendly but insistent demands. He also impressed us with his daring ideas, his fabulous memory, and last but not least with his unusually great working capacity. His insomnia troubled him, but also gave him many extra hours for work and reading. On the other hand, there was something in Hevesy's personality which remained a mystery through all the years I knew him. He was remote and unapproachable as a human being. He surrounded himself with a shield of conventionality which very few of his friends were able to penetrate. Moreover, he did not make an effort to get to know his associates as human beings, he took no interest in their personal fate, although when asked for it, he was always willing to help, for example by writing carefully worded recommendations.

During the thirties the political situation in Europe and its consequences for a large number of people as well as the threat of war were the dominant topics of discussion everywhere. But even in this connection Hevesy displayed a detached, impersonal, and very unemotional attitude. To me, this seemed strange behaviour. After all, Hevesy had left Germany because of the Nazis. He never said a word about his own situation. Rumors would have it that the reason for his departure from Freiburg was "a Jewish grandmother". As many will remember, during the Hitler regime in Germany, "a Jewish grandmother" was like a collective code, or a measuring unit, in which a group of people's undesirability, their chance for escape or survival, could be expressed. "A Jewish grandmother" was the misfortune that had befallen many a distinguished family whose members did not consider themselves Jewish – neither in a religious nor in a "racial" sense. Apparently, Hevesy belonged to this group. He did not want to be mistaken for a person who had left Germany because of "race", rather, that he had taken this step because he was definitely opposed to the vulgar Nazi regime and its atrocities.

At the same time, he was so pre-occupied with his science that he was prepared to ignore a co-worker's or a colleague's political orientation as long as he found his work interesting or useful. This dualism became apparent within the group of scientific associates who joined Hevesy in the second half of the thirties. Among them were a few black sheep. One of them carried the swastica under the lapel of his coat, another later was unmasked as a spy for the Nazis, and a third aired such outspoken sympathies for the Third Reich that one wondered whether Hevesy ever talked with him about anything except the experiments they were performing together. I once went to Hevesy and complained about the uneasiness and embarrassment I felt in this company, but he brushed my concern aside: I should not pay any attention to this foolishness of my colleagues. He did not think it was worth troubling him with such matters.

During this period, a large number of refugee scientists came to the institute for longer or shorter periods seeking help and encouragement from Bohr. Between them existed the intangible and hardly ever verbally expressed recognition of a common fate. In this sometimes tense and troubled atmosphere, Hevesy appeared always unconcerned, almost superficial, pretending that he, personally, had no part in this drama. However, as I found out recently, this was not true; he was involved both on behalf of a few close friends whom he tried to help, and probably even more so in anticipation of his own and his family's future. It is astounding how well he was able to conceal this conflict behind the mask of his conventional attitude, his detachment, and his sarcasm.

An attempt at describing Hevesy's personality at the time he was about 50 years old would be incomplete without a few words about his sense of humor or, rather, the lack of it. I have never heard Hevesy laugh. He appreciated good stories and he told innumerable anecdotes, mainly about people from the world of science. But he had no sense for sharing any kind of fun or gaiety. His kind of humor was part irony, part sarcasm; he did not at all like being himself the subject of a good story. Nobody ever dared to make him the butt of a joke. On the other hand, he provided the essence of countless anecdotes about himself owing to his absent-mindedness, his sometimes surprising reactions, and his linguistic confusion. His associates must bear the blame for not having collected and preserved the hilarious Hevesy stories that cheered and amused the first generation of radio-isotopists all over the world.

My part in the intriguing project Hevesy had initiated was fascinating. The building of instruments and later their continuous adaptation to new tasks was entirely left to me under O. R. Frisch's supervision. Since Hevesy continued to travel often and for weeks at a time, he used to outline a plan of research and to provide the necessary samples, for example the rare earths, for me to work with; on his return he expected to find the work done and the results properly written up. This was an excellent education for a fledgling scientist.

Until the summer of 1935 most of our time and effort was devoted to studies of induced radioactivity. The production of radio-phosphorus, P-32, began slowly, since most neutron sources first were used for physics experiments, and later were placed into the large flask with carbon disulphide. Thus, before the production of radio-phosphorus started, the sources had lost considerably in strength. About every fortnight, Hevesy would extract the P-32 formed by chemical means. Nevertheless the work with radio-phosphorus grew steadily in the course of 1936; thereafter it expanded dramatically. Hevesy was impatient, he had plenty of ideas but the availability of neutron sources depended upon the Radium Station in Copenhagen whose doctors used most of the radon for the treatment of cancer patients. New sources were forthcoming only once in a while, sometimes at intervals of a couple of weeks. Hevesy hated to wait. In the summer of 1935 he had an excellent idea: if the institute owned a radium-beryllium source which has a constant strength (Ra having a half-life of 1600 years) it would make the work independent of the deliveries of sources from the Radium Station. Hevesy talked to some influential people and suggested that Bohr on his 50th birthday should be presented with a large sum of money enabling him to purchase one gram of radium. This plan did materialize: funds were raised all over Denmark and 100,000 Kr. were presented to Bohr in October 1935. Two Ra-Be sources were ordered from the firm Radium Belge but they were not ready for use in Copenhagen until the summer of 1936.

Although the quantities of radio-phosphorus Hevesy could extract from the irradiated carbon disulphide were exeedingly small – always less than one microCurie in each portion – he managed to initiate many different investigations. He did not have a laboratory properly equipped for animal experiments nor sufficient knowledge and experience to perform this kind of work on his own. He therefore established contact with at least half a dozen different research centers in Copenhagen, besides the laboratory of animal physiology of August Krogh who from the start had shown special interest in the application of the indicator method to biological problems. As I have already mentioned, Hevesy could be most persuasive, his enthusiasm was irresistable, and he succeeded in winning his colleagues' collaboration. He was, in fact, an excellent "salesman" of his new technique. Very soon he made experiments on plants at the Carlsberg Laboratory, on muscle at the Physiology Department, on teeth at the School of Dentistry, and on membrane permeability with Krogh, to name just a few.

Since these activities were scattered all over town, it necessarily meant carrying active samples and pieces of equipment around, – but Hevesy was not disturbed by such minor technicalities. When the radium-beryllium sources had been delivered to the institute he decided on an experiment that involved the irradiation of wheat seedlings at the Carlsberg Laboratory. Hevesy wrapped one of the radium-beryllium sources in old newspapers and took the streetcar to the west side of the city. He carefully placed his valuable and strongly radioactive parcel on the rear platform of the streetcar and took a seat near the opposite platform, however keeping a watchful eye on his parcel. As he reached his destination, he picked it up and walked the rest of the way. I never learnt whether the source was carried back to the institute via the same route.

But "salesmanship" alone cannot bring about the enormous expansion and within a short time also the general recognition of a new method. Additional ingredients are needed, for example intellectual support and acceptance in the scientific community, co-workers in the laboratory, and – last but not least – funds.

As I have indicated earlier, a number of factors combined to make the expansion of Hevesy's activities possible: Niels Bohr did not consider biology a branch of science remote from his own. Quite the contrary. In 1932 Bohr had given a lecture entitled "Light and Life" before a congress of light therapy in Copenhagen, which was the first carefully worded presentation to deal predominantly with the extension of his com- plementarity principle into the life sciences. In Bohr's view it was quite natural that there must be room at his institute for a close contact – even collaboration – between physicists and biologists. While Hevesy approached biological problems from a practical viewpoint, that of the experimental biochemist, Bohr was fascinated by the philosophical aspects common to physics and biology and by the "unity of knowledge". Both were eager to pursue the new possibilities which had arisen through the use of radioactive indicators. The backing and encouragement offered by Bohr was essential, but it was not sufficient for Hevesy's dynamic moves. Large scale funding of his project was needed. Fortunately the Rockefeller Foundation was in a process of re-orientation of their general policy in favour of substantial grants for the biological sciences.

A joint effort to raise funds for Hevesy's activities was considered to be of crucial importance. August Krogh, the wellknown Danish physiologist and enthusiastic supporter of Hevesy's plans, enjoyed the high esteem and confidence of the Rockefeller Foundation. Besides, he was the most qualified to evaluate the importance of the indicator method for biological research. Bohr, on the other hand, argued that the production of radio- isotopes could be enhanced manyfold if, instead of using radon- (or radium-) beryllium sources, bombardment was performed in a high volt- age accelerator or, especially, in a cyclotron like the one that had been built a few years earlier by Ernest Lawrence in Berkeley. Thus, the construction of these machines at the institute would be of immense value for Hevesy and also for the physicists who wanted to study nuclear reactions and transformations by means of accelerated particles.

After many consultations, both personal and by letters, with the directors of the Rockefeller Foundation, several versions of the project outline were drafted by Bohr, Hevesy, and Krogh. A detailed description of the project, entitled "physico-biological studies" and an application for funds were submitted to the Foundation. The final document was signed by Bohr alone.

The grant was approved rather promptly and went to Bohr whose prestige in the eyes of the Foundation was the highest. Clearly, Hevesy would direct the work with indicators, Krogh indirectly assured that the research was relevant to biology and contributed to the advancement of the field the Rockefeller Foundation wished to promote. A considerable fraction of the grant was earmarked for the construction of a cyclotron which, in turn, was to be used to a large extent for the production of radio-isotopes for Hevesy and his associates. The rest of the grant secured salaries for two assistants: the first to join the group was the Danish chemist O. Rebbe and the second was L. Hahn from Czechoslovakia; it covered the expenditures for Hevesy's experiments over a period of 5 years.

Now, the conditions were established for Hevesy's research activities during the years that followed. In fact, the Rockefeller Foundation continued to support the tracer work in Copenhagen for many years to come, even after Hevesy had settled permanently in Sweden in the early fifties.

Before I report on Hevesy's work and life during the 5-year period until the German occupation of Denmark in April 1940 it seems worthwhile to return for a moment to the year 1920 when Hevesy left Hungary empty-handed. He had no job and no definite plans for his future. Coming to Copenhagen meant resuming contact with recent progress in atomic physics and being close to Bohr's inspiring and encouraging influence. Hevesy responded immediately and soon was on his way towards new and important investigations. As we have seen, in the early 1920ies he discovered the element hafnium and established one more decisive proof of the validity of Bohr's theory.

In 1934 the situation was different in many respects, but there were also some noteworthy similarities. Hevesy was not empty-handed. In the intervening years he had become a well-known scientist and there were

G. Hevesy lecturing at Bohr's institute ca. 1936. Courtesy: the Niels Bohr Archive.

other openings for him besides Copenhagen – had he been interested. On the other hand, his Freiburg period had not yielded much that was new or scientifically spectacular. Hevesy was on his way to becoming an established professor who followed the traditional pattern of teaching and supervising his students, a situation typical of the German professor beyond his prime. He did not really expect to make another great contribution to science – much less to cause some kind of scientific revolution that would change the direction in which the life sciences developed in the years to come. Rather, he considered himself to be beyond the age of the productive scientist. After his short visit with Bohr in the summer of 1933 he expressed this indirectly to Paneth (25 August 1933) with the words "Ich fand Bohr grossartiger und grösser als je. Die meisten Menschen wachsen nicht mehr wenn sie die Vierziger erreicht haben, Seine fabelhafte Persönlichkeit entwickelte sich immer weiter und weiter" (cf. p. 72) Hevesy's re-union with Bohr triggered a new start. Bohr's excitement about the latest development in nuclear physics and his eagerness to see the Copenhagen group of experimentalists contribute to this field induced Hevesy to perform the experiments with artificial radioactivity of the rare earths. The step from there to the application of radioactive indicators to biological research was not so very large. It is therefore justified to maintain that in the mid thirties the scientific climate at Bohr's institute in Copenhagen again inspired Hevesy to move ahead. There can be little doubt that his achievements during the thirties had a much more profound effect on the development of the sciences than those of the twenties.

From the publication of his first letter to *Nature* in September 1935 until the outbreak of the war in 1939, Hevesy published 25 papers on biological topics besides a dozen general essays on his method and its applicability. As early as December 1936 he mentioned to Paneth that he wanted to write a book on isotopic indicators – both the heavy and the radioactive ones – outlining in detail what this book should contain. Undoubtedly he would have started but for the trouble he and Paneth had with the translation into English and the publication of their textbook on radioactivity which finally appeared in 1938. The book on radioactive indicators had to wait until after the war. During the early years of his biological studies with the aid of isotopes, Hevesy must have lived in a state of elation as he tried to choose between the score of important problems which the indicator method could help to solve. Twelve papers appeared in 1940 and by the end of the war, although his activities were impeded considerably, he had published about 20 more. Even if we take into account that Hevesy usually wrote two or three times about each subject, discussing his results in different languages or at different levels of specialization, the fact remains that he had turned his attention to about 20 topics ranging from general to animal and plant physiology via biochemistry to odontology and medicine. He later moved on to studies of the effect of X-rays on the biochemistry of cancer. This prolificness was not new, he had written just as diligently about hafnium and related subjects. His bibliography lists 50 titles during the first decade (1910-20) and around one hundred during the second (1920-30), not including the books he had published in the course of these years. This kind of statistics is of course superficial and objectionable, it serves no other purpose except to illustrate that Hevesy had no difficulties nor restraints in communicating his scientific ideas to his fellow scientists or, for that matter, to interested laymen. This was in striking contrast to Bohr, who laboured over every sentence and re-wrote each paper many times. It was also in striking contrast to Hevesy's incommunicative attitude towards people outside his scientific circle.

Those were indeed very exciting years. Hevesy's vision about the applicability of radioactive indicators and his vigor in promoting their use is well illustrated by the "international physico-biological conference" held at the institute in Copenhagen in the spring af 1938. Several prominent guests were invited and lectures were given by Joseph and Dorothy Needham (Cambridge), Joseph Parnas (Lwow) and Otto Meyerhof (Heidelberg) besides Krogh and Hevesy himself, – each speaking about their special field of interest. Many foreign and Danish scientists participated in the discussions. It was Hevesy's first exhortation to the international scientific community, drawing attention to this important new method and seeking to bring together researchers with different scientific orientations so they could share their anticipations and experiences. As was to be expected, the 1938 Copenhagen meeting was the first of a great many large and small conferences to be held in the following three decades all over the world. All centered on the use of radio-isotopes and the fantastic progress that was made in following up Hevesy's pioneer work.

A detailed discussion of the wide range of our activities would lead far beyond the scope of this biography; it may even be regarded as unnecessary because Hevesy himself wrote so extensively, also presenting his main topics in general survey articles. Around 1960 he decided to publish a collection in two volumes of what he considered his most important papers. They are arranged in about 10 groups, the headlines of which indicate the gradual change of his interests from the earliest period till the latest, when the tracer method had become a research tool used in many science laboratories all over the world.

The first 4 topics listed under "Life Sciences" in Hevesy's "Adventures in Radioisotope Research" are: Skeleton – Phosphatides – Permeability – Labelled Blood Corpuscles. These titles cover most of the work done in the first 10 years (1935-45) after Hevesy had started to use radio-phosphorous. The results of the pioneer experiments – as described on p. 80 – focused on the dynamic processes occurring in bone. Many turnover studies in other organs were made; they confirmed the interpretation Hevesy had suggested from the very beginning. I recall especially the laborious and time consuming work on teeth showing the difference in phosphate uptake between dentine and enamel. The quantities of radio-phosphorus at our disposal were so small that the activity found in the enamel of a rat's or a cat's teeth was hardly detectable. We measured these samples relative to the counter's natural background for hours, sometimes for days, in order to make sure that they were different from zero. Here again we have reason to marvel at the patience and persistence with which these studies were carried out although they dangerously approached the limit of what was feasible.

These trying experiments also had their amusing moments: I recall our excitement when the P-32 injected cat suddenly escaped; she jumped out of the window and disappeared in the nearby park. Everybody rushed out to retrieve the precious animal. Several wild beasts were caught and wipe tests of their saliva were placed under a Geiger counter – alas in vain! After hours of chasing, the right cat was found and the experiment could proceed in an orderly manner.

The phosphatide group of investigations centered on the route of formation and the turnover of these organic compounds in the organism. The planning of the experiments required a proper understanding of biochemistry, which Hevesy gained within a surprisingly short time. When the Rockefeller Foundation grant came into effect and he had a chance to hire two assistants, he chose two chemists. Also in this group of investigations we find an example of Hevesy's flair for picking one of the important issues, namely nucleic acid formation. In the late thirties he was able to show by means of P-32 that the turnover of DNA is high in the spleen and in the intestinal mucosa of the rat. He assumed that this is due to the high rate of cell production, or protein metabolism, in these organs.

Towards the end of the thirties a few foreign visitors joined the group, some coming from the United States. Our own laboratories were then populated with a variety of experimental animals which the group had learned to take care of without assistance from other laboratories. Our favorites were rabbits which were easier to handle than mice and rats. These peaceful animals are at the heart of one of the "Hevesy classics" told over and over again: one late afternoon Hevesy came rushing down the stairs – obviously he was late, as usual, for some appointment. As he met his assistant on the stairway he exclaimed "Herr Hahn, Herr Hahn, you are lucky, you have your rabbits, – I must go home to my family". This story must not be misunderstood: Hevesy was very fond of his family, his youngest daughter, Pia, had just been born, – but nevertheless, he was a little envious that Herr Hahn could stay in the laboratory through most of the night.

The papers collected under the heading "Permeability" illustrate even better how an entirely new field is opened up as a new technique becomes available. Permeable or semi-permeable membranes play a very important role in living organisms. Every single cell is contained in a membrane. Until Hevesy developed the indicator method, it had not been possible to study in detail the movements of ions and molecules across these membranes. It is therefore easy to imagine that permeability studies – in the widest sense of the term – were in the center of interest after the introduction of isotopic indicators. Krogh and his pupils, first and foremost Hans H. Ussing, were especially interested in membrane permeability. They frequently used the skin of a frog, a membrane which regulates the passage of water, of salts, and also of larger molecules both inward and outward between the organism and the surrounding water. Krogh and Hevesy began their collaboration immediately after Hevesy's arrival in Copenhagen using heavy water, but Krogh recognized early that the usefulness of radioactive isotopes would far exceed that of deuterium as an indicator.

Also the membrane surrounding red blood corpuscles is permeable to many substances, and Hevesy showed that blood corpuscles take up and incorporate labelled phosphate both when it is injected into the organism and when corpuscles are incubated with radioactive phosphate outside the organism. If corpuscles labelled in vitro are re-injected into the blood stream, they will immediately mix with the entire quantity of circulating blood. From the degree of dilution of labelled with unlabelled corpuscles, the total blood volume can be calculated. This study, more than any other investigation Hevesy published, aroused the interest of medical people; they soon realized that the application of the indicator method would not be limited to basic research and would thereby benefit the medical sciences. Clearly, the usefulness of the method in diagnosing disease was anticipated at an early stage. All that was needed to introduce the indicator technique in the hospitals was larger quantities of radioactive material. To this end the construction of the high voltage machine and the cyclotron was pursued energetically at the institute. The first neutron bombardments in the cyclotron to produce radio-phosphorus (1938) yielded samples of moderate strength and purity, – not enough to satisfy Hevesy's needs. So he decided to inquire whether his friend Lawrence in Berkeley, the inventor of the cyclotron, could spare a little radio-phosphorus. Lawrence was most accommodating and shipped by airmail letter a small quantity of a white powder – sodium phosphate – the activity of which was about one milliCurie, a thousand times more than the one microCurie we had been able to make with the radon-beryllium sources. Hevesy was jubilant! Here finally, he had enough P-32 to run all the experiments he had in mind, and he could use a higher activity in each, so that the measurements required less time. It cannot come as a surprise that the number of problems to be investigated and the number of papers to be written increased a great deal. Fortunately, also the group of co-workers grew. The airmail letter shipments from Berkeley mostly handled by Martin D. Kamen continued till the outbreak of the war made this impossible.

The year 1939 brought more unrest and tension, the threat of war was imminent. Slowly, our guests from abroad decided to return home; contact with colleagues in other countries became increasingly difficult. For a short period, Hevesy resumed work with heavy isotopes. Urey had succeeded in preparing the "heavy" oxygen and "heavy" nitrogen isotopes from the naturally occurring mixture of these elements' different isotopes. He made some of this material available for Hevesy who used it immediately for experiments on corn. But Hevesy did not have the equipment for analyzing the samples and started to collect information on how and where to buy a mass spectrometer. For a period of some months the tripartite collaboration between Urey in Chicago, Rudolf Schönheimer at Columbia in New York, and Hevesy was established, and Schönheimer went out of his way to help Hevesy with these analyses. The German occupation of Denmark and Schönheimer's tragic death put an end to these activities.

Even in the fall of 1939 Hevesy appeared unaffected by the turmoil around him; he continued to display the same detached attitude – nobody had any notion that he was deeply disturbed. However, I found a remark in his correspondence with Paneth (14 July 1936) which shows that Hevesy did worry. He wrote "Recently I have pondered repeatedly whether – out of regard for my children – it would have been better if I had settled in the United States and left Europe and her unfriendly tendencies." The letter continues "But, after all, we cannot foresee the future, and my children are of half Danish descent. Whether they will have very great difficulties later – I am not quite convinced."* This is the only mention I

*14 July 1936 to Paneth
"Ich habe mir in der letzten Zeit wiederholt überlegt ob es – mit Rücksicht auf meine Kinder nicht richtiger gewesen wäre mich in den USA niederzulassen und Europa und ihre unfreundlichen Strömungen zu verlassen. Aber schliesslich kann man die Zukunft doch nicht voraussehen und meine Kinder sind zur Hälfte dänischer Abstammung. Ob sie später sehr grosse Schwierigkeiten haben werden, davon bin ich nicht ganz überzeugt".

have found of the word "Abstammung" in relation to his own family. Did he fear that – in case Germany came to dominate Denmark – his children might be in trouble because of their "Jewish" father?

Among the documents from the thirties I also found several letters Hevesy wrote in order to help Stefan Meyer whose future was of real concern to him. The Nazis had dismissed him from his position as the head of the Vienna Radium Institute, forbidden him to enter the laboratories and confiscated his savings. He moved to his house in the country where he lived rather isolated and with modest means. Hevesy tried hard and impatiently to find a position abroad for Stefan Meyer, turning to several influential friends and acquaintances for help, but without success. It seems that Stefan Meyer was not too eager to leave his country; his age and his very poor hearing made him feel insecure about being uprooted. Fortunately, he survived all hardships during the war. Hevesy re-established contact with him as soon as this became possible. They did not meet again, but Hevesy repeatedly expressed in writing his fond memories of the Vienna period and his gratitude to the "great old man" of the Vienna Radium Institute and the famous "Vienna school".

V. M. Goldschmidt also caused Hevesy great concern. Following their close collaboration in the twenties on the hafnium content of various minerals and related topics, they had remained in close contact. While Hevesy was professor in Freiburg, Goldschmidt had accepted a professorship in Göttingen (1929) where he stayed until the Nazi regime forced him to leave. Before he could regain his Norwegian citizenship and his position at the University of Oslo, Goldschmidt encountered many personal and economic problems and Hevesy tried to help. A few years later, Goldschmidt again became a victim of the Nazis in Norway, but he managed to escape to England. He decided to return to Oslo after the war, but he was a sick, unhappy man and he died from heart failure in 1947. Ever since they had met early in their careers, Hevesy had admired Goldschmidt for his almost boundless energy and his profound knowledge in geochemistry; he felt sympathy for a man who, time and again, was unhappy and on bad terms with his colleagues.

In the summer of 1939, the Rockefeller Foundation invited Hevesy to the United States, suggesting that he visit – as a consultant – a number of

American laboratories where isotopic indicators were being introduced. The trip was to take place early in 1940. He wrote about this to Paneth (22 July 1939) and in the same letter, he mentioned an offer he had received (confidentially) from India. He remarked regretfully that he would have preferred an offer from Canada, saying that "Consideration of the world-political situation could bring me to leave Denmark, but India – no."* Such a move would almost certainly have been a serious threat to his health.

Again – as in previous years – Hevesy kept his worries to himself and played the role of the well-balanced, but also good humoured fatalist. But after the German occupation of Denmark on April 9, 1940, even Hevesy was driven close to despair. He did not show it, but more than 40 years later, the correspondence between Hevesy and Urey came to my attention, and I then learnt that Hevesy had made desperate attempts at securing passage to the United States for himself and his wife. From America, both Urey and the Rockefeller Foundation sent him new invitations to various conferences and lecture tours, which should have served as a suitable pretext to bring him over. To Hevesy's great dismay all his efforts to obtain passage on a boat or on the trans-Siberian railroad failed. He was trapped in Denmark – at least for some time. Now it is impossible to find out whether or not Hevesy spoke to Bohr about his fears and his intention to leave Denmark for the U.S. If he did, Bohr never mentioned their conversation to anybody now alive.

Until the summer of 1943, the situation in Denmark, the day-by-day life of ordinary people, remained almost unchanged and peaceful, especially as compared to the life of people in some other occupied countries, such as Norway or the Netherlands. But then, the political climate changed drastically, and in the fall the action planned by the Nazis against the Jews in Denmark was revealed through indirect diplomatic channels. This provoked the well-known and widely documented rescue of the Danish Jews by a united Danish population. In the course of 2-3 weeks a few thousand people were brought to safety across the Sound, the narrow

*22 July 1939 to Paneth
"Rücksichten auf die weltpolitische Lage würde mich dazu bringen, Dänemark zu verlassen, aber Indien – nein".

strait which separates Denmark from Sweden. Warnings that Bohr and his family were in great danger came at the same time. Not primarily because Bohr was half-Jewish and an atomic scientist, but rather because the Germans knew that he was an ardent and influential opponent of the Nazi regime. Bohr was strongly urged by his friends and advisers to give up his stern refusal to leave his country – which he had insisted upon until this moment. He was brought to Sweden the last day of September 1943 and a few days later he was flown to England.

I was helped to safety across the Sound and was immediately offered work and a modest emergency salary at the University of Stockholm. During the weeks that followed, many Swedish scientists were actively engaged in helping their Danish colleagues by preparing for their employment even before some of the Danes had actually arrived. To the best of my knowledge, nobody expected that Hevesy might feel the threat of prosecution, he had never shown his concern. However, in mid-October, Hevesy appeared in Stockholm. Since he had an Hungarian passport, he simply boarded a train in Copenhagen. He came alone and without luggage but he had no intention to go back. Just as in the thirties he did not say a word about his personal situation.

Hevesy did not need the assistance of various committees and organizations which had been formed in order to help the refugees from Denmark who came without their belongings and most of them without money. He had his close friend Hans v. Euler with whom he had conducted experiments on Jensen sarcomas in rats since the beginning of 1941. For almost three years, letters and samples had been sent back and forth every week. Since early in 1943 every single letter had been opened by the censor. Certainly, Hevesy found this kind of collaboration cumbersome and preferred to join Euler at his Institute for Organic Chemistry in Stockholm. It was less fortunate that his "lieber und sehr verehrter Freund" – as they addressed each other in writing – had shown great sympathy for the German Reich. Both within and outside university circles many resented v. Euler's openly pro-German orientation. I have stated earlier that Hevesy was not interested in a colleague's political views as long as scientific co-operation was desirable and productive. His close affiliation with v. Euler illustrates this point.

Although Hevesy worked at the Institute of Organic Chemistry and I was at the Wennergren Institute of Experimental Biology, we met frequently. Hevesy's family arrived eventually, and they settled in some provisional living quarters, later in a beautiful apartment. Just as he had done in Copenhagen, Hevesy soon established contact and collaboration with several laboratories which he visited regularly although, even in Sweden, the war situation slowed down all scientific activities. In the Swedish scientific community Hevesy was met with the respect and friendliness he deserved. Radioactive indicators had made him very well known first of all among all who worked in the life sciences and basic medical research.

In the fall of 1944 the news that Hevesy had been awarded the Nobel Prize in chemistry for the year 1943 was received with great joy and satisfaction by everybody everywhere. At last, Hevesy had been found deserving of this prize which is widely considered to be the highest distinction that can be bestowed on a scientist. Hevesy was pleased although he did not seem to attach too much importance to this event. As mentioned earlier, it is my impression that he had not forgotten his disappointment with the Swedish Academy of Science who failed to honor him for the discovery of hafnium. The prize was also a welcome support at a time of economic uncertainties. Moreover, every laureate has the option to become a Swedish citizen. In rare cases only is this offer of real interest to a laureate, but Hevesy did accept it; he exchanged his Hungarian passport for a Swedish one.

# Nobel Prize and World Fame

The award of the Nobel Prize signaled another turning point in Hevesy's life: it almost coincided with the end of the Second World War which marked the end of an epoch, or rather the beginning of a new one, also in science. The concentrated effort, mainly in the United States, to control and to exploit the process of nuclear fission profoundly affected the scientific situation in many fields besides physics and technology. For example, the large scale production of radio-isotopes in nuclear reactors caused a decisive change from the classical working methods used by Hevesy towards a new technology. In a reactor, radioactive isotopes of any element in the periodic system could be produced in quantities that far exceeded the demand one might expect from research laboratories. At the same time, new apparatuses had been developed in which highly active material could be measured. In other words, the indicator method could now be used on a much larger scale, and the primitive instruments of the pre-war period were replaced by automatic devices. Radio-isotopes were soon produced commercially, they became a merchandise, and the equipment needed in isotope work likewise appeared on the market in a variety of designs.

In the first years after the war, the Americans were restrictive with regard to making radioactive material available. When these restrictions were lifted gradually, radio-isotopes became accessible to research laboratories – and soon also to hospitals – in the United States and in Europe. Hevesy received shipments which he used both in Copenhagen and in Stockholm. The isotope carbon-14 with a half-life of about 5500 years, discovered by Martin Kamen, became the most important tool for biological studies. The possibility of "labelling" large organic molecules with a radioactive carbon isotope in many different positions opened new avenues of research. It is no exaggeration to say that molecular biology could not have advanced so rapidly without the use of radio-carbon.

Hevesy was confronted with new personal problems when the war ended: where was he going to live and work in the future? In his correspondence with colleagues and co-workers in Copenhagen, he repeatedly assured them that he would return shortly; this undoubtedly was his intention at that time.

Bohr came back to Denmark from the United States, where he had been for almost two years, with many plans for the future. He wanted to enlarge his institute in order to provide room for more extensive experimental as well as theoretical work in nuclear physics. He also wished to bring scientists from many countries – east and west – to Copenhagen, to re-establish contacts, and to work towards international understanding and openness through scientific collaboration.

It also became clear that biological isotope work would not be resumed in the same fashion it had been carried out during the thirties. Many Danish biologists thought that this type of work should be brought into its proper environment, which meant from a physics institute to the biology division of the university. The emphasis should not be on the previous "physico-biological" but on biological studies. It is my impression that August Krogh was the "primus motor" in these endeavours. Although he was due to retire soon, he eagerly pursued his efforts to make the isotope group a part of his own institute, the Zoophysiological Laboratory. His viewpoints certainly were not in conflict with Bohr's, who always had emphasized the close links between physics and biology but hardly thought that he could provide optimal working conditions for biological studies at his Institute of Theoretical Physics. Maybe Bohr also foresaw that the realization of his own plans would make a simultaneous expansion of Hevesy's group at his institute problematic. However, he assured Hevesy that there would always be room in the new premises – although it was to be expected that isotope application would become much more diversified and hence would need considerably larger facilities and financial support.

Soon after the liberation of Denmark, Krogh travelled to Stockholm in order to discuss these matters with Hevesy and he also came to see me; he

G. Hevesy when he was awarded the Nobel Prize in 1944. Courtesy: the Niels Bohr Archive.

asked whether I would be willing to join his Zoophysiological Laboratory, bringing along some of the old equipment. It was to be my task not only to continue my research but moreover – as a physicist – to teach biologists how to work with radioactive isotopes. I accepted Krogh's offer without hesitation. His views about the future placement of biological isotope work were convincing – I expected them to be shared by Bohr – and I saw the opportunity for a permanent position at the university in Copenhagen after 10 years of dependence on fellowships.

After the German occupation and the end of the war, the situation in Denmark – as in most of Europe – was one of great confusion. Shortage of all kinds of material, economic chaos, and changes in the traditionally stable social order followed. Clearly, it would take quite some time to re-establish normal living and working conditions. The very first steps towards a re-location of the isotope work were not taken until the spring of 1946. Hevesy's plans for the future also had to be adjusted to the slowly emerging possibilities at the universities of Copenhagen and of Stockholm. He decided to wait and in any case to stay in Stockholm for the winter of 1945-46, hoping that some economic support for his work would be forthcoming.

The Rockefeller Foundation had continued to finance the physico-biological project in Copenhagen until America entered the war. From then on, and for several years to come, the Danish Carlsberg Foundation took over this commitment including the salaries of Hevesy's assistants K. Zerahn and J. Ottesen who had started in the early forties and continued their research after Hevesy had left for Sweden. In fact the Carlsberg Foundation supported their work until new arrangements had been made, thus facilitating the gradual transfer of the isotope group to the Zoophysiological Laboratory in the course of the second half of the 1940ies. After Krogh had retired – establishing however a small laboratory in his private home – he travelled to the United States; on his own and Bohr's behalf he tried to persuade the Rockefeller Foundation to renew the grant for the Copenhagen group. Together with Bohr, Krogh's successor, Paul Brandt Rehberg, negotiated this agreement which first came into effect in 1949; it then continued for many years.

Early in 1946 Hevesy approached the Rockefeller Foundation asking them to renew the support of his trip to the United States which he had had to cancel when the war broke out in 1939. He finally made this trip in the spring of 1947; eight years had passed between his previous planning of a visit and his arrival in the U.S. Now, he was no longer to be the consultant for the American beginners in the field of radioactive indicators; rather, he wanted to see and learn what research centers in the United States were doing with the abundant supply of radioactive "tracers" – the term now frequently used instead of Hevesy's "indicators" – and with their advanced instrumentation. Hevesy also saw with some amazement that isotopes were used extensively in hospitals both for diagnostic purposes and for therapy. Although the American scientists had moved ahead both technically and scientifically, Hevesy was duly honored and celebrated everywhere as the originator of a unique idea with far-reaching consequences and a pioneer in applying the results of nuclear physics to biological studies.

After his return from this visit to America, Hevesy came to Copenhagen often and, encouraged by Bohr, he played with the idea of working on chemical problems in Copenhagen and concentrating his biological research in Stockholm (letter to Bohr, 27 May 1946). At the same time, Bohr's plans to enlarge the institute materialized, and young scientists from other countries began to arrive in Copenhagen to work at his institute.

During this period of indecision Hevesy began to write the textbook on radioactive indicators he had planned almost ten years earlier. This book – dedicated to his friend and promotor August Krogh – appeared in 1948 and is the classical text on the production, measurement, and application of isotopes as tracers. Hevesy adhered to the outline he had discussed with Paneth. As I have indicated, the development of the tracer technique proceeded so rapidly that Hevesy's text soon became outdated. Nevertheless, this presentation of his ideas and his method is a historical document showing his broad approach to the field from the very beginning in Manchester and Vienna. In the course of the 1950ies and 60ies radioactive tracers became a tool equally widespread and indispensable in the laboratory as, say, a microscope.

G. Hevesy and August Krogh during Krogh's visit in Stockholm 1945.
Courtesy: the Hevesy family.

One after the other, Hevesy's Danish co-workers moved from Bohr's institute to the Zoophysiological Laboratory, and his influence on their work faded slowly, although he visited us at intervals and always was most interested and willing to discuss our research. These visits frequently took place when Hevesy was travelling anyway. By that time, Hevesy had settled in Stockholm permanently. Besides the scientific situation in Copenhagen and in Stockholm, Hevesy had also considered the well-being of his children when he made his decision. He did not want to uproot them a third time from their school and the environment they cherished. His oldest daughter, Jenny, had finished her school years in Stockholm and, as soon as travelling again became possible, she went to England and stayed for a longer period with the Paneth family. His son, George, neared the final school examination and wanted to study medicine. The two younger daughters, Ingrid and Pia, still went to school. Mrs. Hevesy, although born in Denmark, very much liked Stockholm where living conditions at that time were much better than in Denmark. She did not advocate the family's return to Copenhagen.

Once more, the two volumes of "Adventures in Radioisotope Research" can serve as a guide to Hevesy's work towards the end of his active research period. Studies of red blood corpuscles, of bone, and of iron metabolism were continued, but the main emphasis was on radiation biology, an interest he shared with v. Euler. The effect of X-rays on nucleic acid formation and closely related problems were analyzed in many investigations and are discussed in numerous papers. Radio-carbon labelled compounds had become a useful tool; they were available commercially at high activity levels. After v. Euler's retirement, Hevesy performed most of his work at the Karolinska Institution together with the hematologist Dieter Lockner who became the co-author of all his original papers between 1962 and 1965.

Hevesy was almost 60 years old when he was awarded the Nobel Prize; he remained an active and productive scientist for two more decades. Honors and prizes were heaped upon him. He received honorary degrees, memberships of learned societies, medals, and invitations to international conferences which could be made into big events thanks to the attendance of the Nobel laureate. There seemed to be no end to the opportunities for travel and celebration. However, all this glamour was not to Hevesy's taste. His insomnia plagued him and his desire to travel had diminished; especially he disliked travelling long distances by air. This kind of social life had become too strenuous. For several years, his health had been a brake on his constant urge to be active and it began to trouble him more seriously in his seventies.

As I have described previously, Hevesy considered himself to be "of age" as early as in the late 1920ies when he was about 40 years old. He went to Freiburg because he did not expect to be scientifically productive much longer, and it was time for him to begin a career as a teacher. At the age of 50 he returned to Copenhagen and began his work in biology. He was indeed capable of familiarizing himself thoroughly with a new field, and in the course of the following 10 years, his scientific career reached a second climax. It can hardly be disputed that his accomplishments in developing and applying the tracer method to biological problems had a much greater, a more far-reaching impact on many different branches of science than his discovery of hafnium in the twenties. Thanks to Hevesy, basic research in the life sciences could tackle problems which had not been accessible before; also chemical technology profited enormously from the introduction of neutron activation analysis.

In medicine the impact of the new isotope technique was so great that, in the course of the sixties, special departments for "nuclear medicine" were established in most large hospitals the world over. Radio-isotopes were used both to diagnose and also to treat diseases. The first isotopes used extensively in hospitals were phosphorus-32 and iodine-131, the former in connection with erythrema, the latter – because iodine is taken up selectively by the thyroid gland – in diagnosis and treatment of diseases of the thyroid. Radio-iodine emits gamma rays and therefore it can be located and measured by means of a detector placed outside the body; in many cases there is no need to take blood or tissue samples for analysis.

In the 1950ies new instruments were developed which register the gamma radiation from radio-iodine in the thyroid while the detector is moved back and forth over the area to be studied. The instrument draws a chart of the isotope distribution. The next step in instrument perfection led to the so-called gamma camera which depicts the distribution of the radio-isotope inside the organism on a TV-screen. Several methods are now in use which are based on the incorporation of gamma ray emitting isotopes into substances which adhere to, or follow the movement of special compounds in the body. Blood flow, air ventilation, and many other dynamic processes can be monitored in this way without discomfort to the patient. In cancer research and diagnosis radio-isotopes play an important role. Hevesy could hardly have imagined how widely his method would be applied in the field of medicine. It is worth mentioning however, that in some of the techniques just described, Hevesy's basic criterion of chemical identity of the "label" with the "element to be labelled" has been abandoned. For example, in flow studies, the addition of microscopically small labelled particles – which need not be identical with the cells or molecules carried in the stream – will provide a truthful picture of what happens in the process under study. Similarly, a labelled compound which has an affinity or adheres to a certain cell type need not be identical with the cell components, it will nevertheless be an "indicator" of the structure to which it adheres.

Thus, in the field of nuclear medicine, the classical definition of a radioactive tracer as described on page 81 is no longer a "conditio sine qua non" for the application of the tracer method. Today, the concept "tracer method" covers a considerably wider range of radio-isotope application than was envisaged by Hevesy. Still, he is rightly considered the founder of nuclear medicine.

Some outstanding medical researchers were among those who strongly recommended Hevesy as a candidate for the Atoms for Peace Award which he received from the hands of Mr. Dag Hammarskjöld, the Secretary General of the United Nations, in 1959. The medical application of radio-isotopes naturally lagged behind basic biological research by about one decade, and so did the recognition of Hevesy as the great pioneer by the medical profession. This delay was more than compensated for by the veneration for Hevesy expressed in the following years by experts in the field of cancer research and radiobiology.

# Towards the Close of a Long and Active Life

By the end of the 1950ies many of the physicists and chemists Hevesy had known as his teachers and colleagues from the Manchester and Vienna period and even from the Copenhagen circle of the twenties had passed away. He lost his closest friend and confident Fritz Paneth (1958) whom he had known since the early days in Vienna. When Hevesy moved to Copenhagen in the mid thirties, Paneth settled in England and, after 6 years at Imperial College in London, he held the professorship in chemistry in Durham from 1939 until 1953. His scientific interests focused on geochemistry, especially meteorites. In addition, he wrote extensively about historical and philosophical topics. When he retired, his reputation as a scientist with unusually broad cultural interests and undiminished vitality brought him the honor of an invitation to another important post, namely as director of the newly established Max Planck Institute of Chemistry in Mainz, Germany. During the war the close contact between Hevesy and Paneth was interrupted but it was re-established very soon. Aside from many personal matters they eagerly discussed a new and enlarged edition of their textbook on radioactivity, but this plan did not materialize. The correspondance between Hevesy and Paneth during the 1950ies has not yet been found; still, over a period of 40 years they had exchanged hundreds of letters, most of which were preserved by Paneth. These letters convinced me that Paneth was the only friend to whom Hevesy confided his personal problems; he undoubtedly was one of the very few who knew the human being behind the façade Hevesy presented to the large majority of his acquaintances. Although Paneth's family background was different from Hevesy's – Paneth's father was a well-known physiologist in Vienna – they were brought up in the same traditions and had so much in common that there was no reason for Hevesy to pretend or conceal anything during their life-long friendship.

My impressions of Hevesy at the time when we worked together in the 1930ies are described on pp. 82-87: his attitude and his reaction to the political events had seemed strange, almost incomprehensible. Nearly 50 years later, while reading his correspondence, a much more coherent picture of his personality evolved. It became ever clearer that Hevesy, this intelligent and ambitious man, surmounted serious adversities and problems at the cost of his true self. The dichotomy between his true and his assumed identity caused conflicts he was determined to keep to himself. The knowledge of his background helps us better to understand some of the characteristic traits of his personality: his restlessness, his remarkable ability to adapt to drastic changes in his situation, and his capacity to familiarize himself with new scientific domains. Even his irony and his indomitable optimism stem from traditions which, through many generations, had developed in the minority group to which he and his ancestors belonged.

As a result of his turn towards the life sciences, Hevesy made many new friends among biologists and cancer specialists, with whom he had a lively correspondence until his death. Especially, Charles Huggins became his devoted friend. He was the head of the Ben May Laboratory for Cancer Research at the University of Chicago. He was well known for his investigations into the role played by hormones in the development of cancer. Hevesy had met Huggins at a scientific conference in Italy in the later 1950ies and they had established a warm relationship with one another; they corresponded frequently.

Although Hevesy's involvement in experimental work slowed down, he remained a prolific writer. At the same time he began to look back on his own research and on his life. He had already published an autobiographical essay "A Scientific Career" which his friend Huggins had asked him to write. It appeared first in "Perspectives in Biology and Medicine" in 1958 and is indeed typical of his style. He tells exceedingly little about himself and absolutely nothing about his family. By means of episodes and anecdotes he conveys a picture of important people he had met in the course of his life and of events from the world of science with almost chatty eloquence. Many a reader of this essay will gain the impression that Hevesy avoided telling anything about his personal development, his experiences, and his views concerning the serious problems of his time. This, indirectly, confirms the profile I have tried to draw in the previous chapters. Hevesy used these autobiographical notes again a few years later (1962) as an introduction to "Adventures in Radioisotope Research" which I have mentioned before. Fifty years after his first formulation of the principle of radioactive indicators, Hevesy wanted to select from several hundred papers he had written on this topic those he considered to be the most important ones. He also felt the need to comment on some of his earlier work, pointing out shortcomings due to, for example, the limited quantities of radio-isotopes available at that time, or referring to later work which confirmed his assumptions and interpretations.

As I have discussed repeatedly in different contexts, Bohr played a unique role in Hevesy's life ever since the beginning of Hevesy's career as a scientist. Twice he offered him hospitality and a chance for a new start. After the First World War when Hevesy desperately wanted to emigrate from Hungary and find a position abroad, Bohr invited him to Copenhagen and, in the course of a few years, the inspiration Hevesy found at Bohr's institute led to the discovery of element 72, hafnium.

A similar situation arose when Hitler came to power in Germany. Again, Bohr provided the support which made a continuation of Hevesy's research in Copenhagen possible. Without Bohr's active involvement, the fantastic "adventure in radio-isotope research" that brought Hevesy world fame would not have been possible.

The close friendship between Bohr and Hevesy was very important to both. This may appear surprising at first in view of the striking dissimilarity of their personalities. However, quite naturally, each admired in his friend just those qualities that were not his own. Scientifically, Hevesy was an experimentalist, although he was not very skillful in the laboratory. In contrast to Bohr, he was primarily interested in methods, their further development and application, and much less so in theoretical considerations or in biological problems per se. Bohr, one of the great thinkers of

G. Hevesy, Niels Bohr and Mrs. Margrethe Bohr in Manchester 1913. One of their first meetings. Courtesy: the Niels Bohr Archive.

G. Hevesy, Otto Hahn and Niels Bohr at the Lindau meeting of Nobel laureates 1962. The last meeting of Hevesy with Bohr. Courtesy: the Hevesy family.

our time, admired not only Hevesy's comprehensive knowledge in physical chemistry – a field which had developed into a special domain around the turn of the century – but also his flair for the ways in which scientific problems might be solved. Bohr valued the efficiency with which Hevesy handled any situation and appreciated that he was a "doer" who made decisions fast and carried them out promptly. Bohr was very much the opposite: he was shy – actually very shy in his younger years – he needed time and careful consideration before making decisions, he felt warmly for other people and involved himself in their fate, and he made every conceivable effort to help colleagues and friends. In contrast to Hevesy's egocentricity, Bohr was concerned with the problems of the world and his fellow-men, he fought actively for tolerance and under-standing – matters of rather academic interest to Hevesy. Since both were great personalities, they could value the strength and qualities of the other without ever expressing "mutual admiration". Yet, towards the end of his life, Hevesy sometimes gave in to this weakness.

As both men grew older they found occasions to remember their common experiences. In the fall of 1957 Hevesy wrote to Bohr that he had come across some old notes he had written in Hungary in 1923 about the discovery of hafnium and the ensuing controversy. Although there was nothing in these notes that was not well known to Bohr, Hevesy continued "he who some time in the future may describe your life may find in these notes a few episodes of interest" – and therefore he forwarded the notes to Bohr. This remark is worth noting because it touches upon an emotion that later became increasingly important to Hevesy and caused him to write about his own life again.

One year later Hevesy had been leafing through old documents again, and he wrote to Bohr in October 1958: " Recently I had in my hands a number of letters you wrote me in the course of the last 45 years. They speak so much kindness and unique goodwill and helpfulness that I was deeply moved as I re-read them".

Just at that time Bohr was working on his Rutherford Lectures and he hoped that Hevesy would help him revive memories of their Manchester time. Because of Hevesy's poor health this personal meeting did not take place, but in November 1958 Bohr wrote a long letter to his friend, which describes their relationship better than any biographer can do it. It reads:

"At our age, a steadily shrinking circle of colleagues and friends-for-life is left and my thoughts often go back to the great adventure we have experienced together. Just these days as I am preparing a Rutherford Lecture entitled "General implications of the discovery of the atomic nucleus" which I was asked to give before the Physical Society in London on November 28, I am thinking especially of the old days in Manchester where both of us worked under the inspiring influence of Rutherford and formed so close a friendship. For the recollection of memories it has been a great help to read your beautiful paper "A scientific career" in "Perspectives in Biology and Medicine", and it also amused and pleased me very much to read your notes you so kindly sent me concerning the fantastic story of the discovery of hafnium and the response in the world of science.

I was also moved to hear that you re-read our correspondence from the old days and I, myself, have also just re-read it and found many remarks which vividly reminded me of the moods prevailing during these exciting years. In this connection many impressions have also been strengthened by re-reading my correspondence with Rutherford from that time. I do not yet know how much of all this I want to include in my lecture in London. But it may interest you that Rutherford who – with his unique common sense and untiring eagerness for discovery – often expressed himself in a short and practical manner, that he in his last years took a warm interest in the general philosophical viewpoints based on atomic physics. Only a few months before his death I had an unforgettable conversation with him about this.

Yes, we have many beautiful memories in common and share the joy of thinking about the great development we both have seen growing out of the first seed. First of all however, it is the greatest joy to observe how knowledge and understanding grow for every day in the custody of the younger generation. As regards the very youngest, I can report that we just had our 14th grandchild, since a week ago Aage and Marietta* had a daughter they named Margrethe.

* Aage Bohr, Niels Bohr's third son, a physicist, married to Marietta, née Soffer.

116

I sincerely hope that you are feeling quite well again and I am looking forward to our meeting soon so that we can really talk together about the new and the old.

With my kindest regards ... from my home to your home«.

At the death of Niels Bohr in the fall of 1962 Hevesy felt deep grief. He had known Bohr for almost 50 years, he had loved and admired him more than any of his friends, both as a great scientist and a unique human being. He wrote to Huggins on 17 November 1962 "The shocking news of the death of Niels Bohr reached me this morning. What a loss. Centuries may elapse until a man like him will be born. The world became poorer, very much poorer by his death".

About the time of Niels Bohr's death Hevesy's career as an active and productive scientist came to an end. His health was deteriorating, and one of his old friends, Dr. Heilmeyer from the university clinic at Freiburg, whom he consulted, diagnosed a lung cancer. The last years of Hevesy's life were painful not only physically but maybe even more so because he could no longer work and move about as he wanted to. His thoughts began to circle around the memories of his eventful and exceedingly active life and now he found more time for his family, first of all his grandchildren. His son George worked as a physician in Stockholm, he has 2 children. The youngest daughter Pia and her family lived in Geneva with 2 children, the oldest Jenny, married to Gustav Arrhenius, had settled in La Jolla, California; they have 3 children. Ingrid lived in Freiburg. Hevesy returned to America a few times mainly in order to stay for a while in La Jolla where the climate is perfect and where he could enjoy the presence of his family. On these occasions, he belatedly shared with his children recollections of his own childhood, of the life style and the social trends in Austrio-Hungarian society at the turn of the century. He also appreciated the company of many outstanding scientists affiliated with the University of California. His wife Pia travelled with him as his devoted companion.

Although he could not really continue his research activities, Hevesy wanted to remain in personal contact with his fellow scientists; he met them regularly, for example at the annual Nobel laureate meetings in Lindau am Bodensee near the Swiss-German border or the gatherings of the members of the Pour-le-mérite in Bonn, a society for distinguished scientists and artists. In these social re-unions with old friends from the intellectual elite, he found pleasure and relief. Even more than these events he treasured participating in the Pontifical Academy of Science meetings in Rome, where he spoke twice and in June 1963 gave a memorial lecture on Bohr; he was also received by the Pope.

In these last years of his life, Hevesy wrote many letters to Huggins who responded with both admiration and compassion. Although Hevesy at times was almost unable to hold a pen, he continued to report on his failing health and to mention scientific questions he kept turning over in his mind. Hevesy's letters also contain a great many reminescences from his scientific career and his relations to Rutherford and Bohr, told with warmth and sensitivity. His reserved and impersonal attitude of earlier years gave way to an almost affectionate appreciation of those who cared for him. Untiringly Huggins gave advice and encouragement and he tried to cheer Hevesy with gifts and visits. In fact, Hevesy received the attention of a whole team of experts in the field of cancer research; they consulted among themselves on what to do and travelled far in order to visit Hevesy although there was little they could accomplish.

As his situation worsened, Hevesy and his family felt that he could not obtain the necessary hospital care in Stockholm; he therefore accepted an offer from Dr. Heilmeyer and was admitted to his clinic in Freiburg. There he was given the constant medical care he needed, no effort was spared to make his life as tolerable as possible. He celebrated his 80th birthday in Freiburg on 1 August 1965 and received the ovations of innumerable colleagues and friends as well as of many official representatives of the world of science.

The last time he put his thoughts on paper, Hevesy wrote an autobiography which he intended to be the source material for whoever was asked to write his obituary for the Royal Society of London. He sent this essay to John D. Cockcroft – a distinguished member of the Society – and it was published in "Biographical Memoirs of Fellows of the Royal Society" vol. 13, of November 1967. At the end of the obituary, Cockcroft explains: "My account of Hevesy's life and work has been taken almost entirely from the very extensive and detailed notes which he sent to me shortly before his death to be used "by whoever was invited to write his memorial notice"".

A comparison of Hevesy's manuscript which is now at the Niels Bohr Archive with the printed version shows that Cockcroft, prior to publishing these notes, changed the "I-form" Hevesy had used into the "he-form", corrected a few grammatical errors, and omitted some anecdotes and episodes he apparently found excessive. This clearly was not Hevesy's intention: he had written the essay to help a potential biographer, and mainly to collect the facts and events which posterity might want to know about his scientific career. It is perfectly in keeping with the attitude he had always shown, with the omission of everything he regarded as private, and his conviction that he himself knew best what was important. He included in this essay his opinions about political issues, about scientific developments as well as about many individuals and their achievements. In his evaluations, he was quite blunt and did not care in the least what others might think.

The reader of the obituary who assumes that this is a fellow-scientist's appraisal of Hevesy's life and work will have to be alert till he arrives at the very last lines of this long article in order to discover who the author really was. This "biography" is based almost exclusively on Hevesy's memory: in 1962 Fajans asked Hevesy in a letter for some scientific details from the Manchester period. Hevesy answered as best he could and added that he had moved his home altogether 8 times and therefore could not possibly carry all his papers and documents from place to place – he had thrown most of them away. However, he had kept the letters he had received from Rutherford and Bohr and a few other great personalities. While writing, Hevesy relied on references in his earlier publications, which were not always precise; he was seriously ill and had neither the strength nor the opportunity to check the details. Errors were therefore unavoidable. But this is of minor importance as long as the story he told us is understood to be not the result of a scholarly study carried out by a colleague or a historian, but his own picture of himself. As such it is particularly interesting because it is a self-portrait painted with greater detail but with the same brush he had used earlier.

At the end of the obituary we are told that Hevesy visited Rome in the

G. Hevesy in the 1960s. Courtesy: the Hevesy family.

spring of 1966 in order to attend a conference on hematology at the Pontifical Academy and had another personal audience with the Pope. His strong desire to travel to Rome is mentioned repeatedly in his letters; he was prepared to endure considerable strain in order to make this trip. In fact, he was so weak and in danger of suffocation that Dr. Heilmeyer arranged for a medical escort and for travelling facilities which enabled Hevesy to make the journey and to return to Freiburg safely. He died two months later, on 5 July 1966.

Why was it so important for him to take part in the meeting at the Pontifical Academy, and maybe even more important to be received by the Pope? Was he longing to close the circle of his spiritual life where it had begun: under the guidance of a catholic priest? This great – and at the same time mystifying – personality would never let us know; this was, indeed, a very personal matter. His sorrowful remark at the death of his friend Niels Bohr is also true of Hevesy himself: He made the world richer through his devotion to and his important achievements in science. The application of the tracer method to basic science, technology, and especially medicine has enabled scientists to make spectacular progress. It can be stated without reservation that this progress has been to the benefit of mankind.

# References

*Autobiographical Essays Written by Hevesy*
"A Scientific Career" in Perspectives in Biology and Medicine 1958, vol. I, p. 345

the same text as introduction to "Adventures in Radioisotope Research", Pergamon Press 1962

"George de Hevesy, 1885–1966" in Biographical Memoirs of Fellows of the Royal Society, 1967, vol. 13, edited by J. D. Cockcroft

*Books on Background Material*
"Eastern Europe Between the Wars 1918–1941" by H. Seton-Watson, Cambridge University Press 1945

"Chemistry and Beyond", ed. H. Dingle and O. R. Martin.
A selection from the writings of F. A. Paneth, Interscience Publishers 1964

"Illustrious Immigrants" by Laura Fermi, University of Chicago Press 1968

"Radiochemistry and the Discovery of Isotopes" by A. Romer, Dover Publications Inc. N.Y. 1970

"Jewish Nobles and Geniuses in Modern Hungary" by W. O. McCagg jr., East European Quarterly, Boulder, Columbia University Press 1972

"R. Schoenheimer, Isotopic Tracers and Biochemistry", by R. E. Kohler, Hist. Studies Physical Sci. 1977, vol. 8, p. 257

"The Early Years. The Niels Bohr Institute 1921–1930" by P. Robertson, Akademisk Forlag 1979

"Anatomy of a Priority Conflict: Case of Element 72" by H. Kragh, Centaurus 1980, vol. 23, p. 275

*Biographical articles about G. Hevesy*

E. Cremer: "Georg v. Hevesy" in Allgemeine und praktische Chemie 1966, vol. 17, p. 692

V. P. Guinn: "Nuclear Activation Analysis 45 Years after George Hevesy's Discovery" in J. Radioanal. Chem. 1980, vol. 59, p. 309

Hilde Levi: "The Development of the Tracer Method 1935—45" (Greetings to Professor Hevesy on his 80th Birthday), J. Appl. Rad. Isotopes 1965, vol. 16, p. 505

"George de Hevesy. 1 August 1885—5 July 1966" Nucl. Physics 1967, vol. A98, p.1

"George de Hevesy and his Concept of Radioactive Indicators – in Retrospect." George von Hevesy Memorial Lecture, Europ. J. Nucl. Med. 1976 vol. 1, p. 3

W. G. Myers: "G. C. de Hevesy, The Father of Nuclear Medicine" J. Nucl. Med. 1979, vol. 20, p. 590

R. Spence: "George Charles de Hevesy", Chemistry in Britain 1967, vol. 3, p. 527

*Transcription of facsimile on p. 41:*

Gersonsvej 55, Hellerup
Kopenhagen 23-12-19.

My dear Hevesy,

We all thank you so much for your kind Christmas greetings and send in return our very heartiest wishes for a happy new year for you and your relations. We are all looking forward so much to seeing you here in the spring, and I hope we shall succeed in making your stay here a pleasant time for you.

 With kindest regards from my wife and Christian and Hansemand and myself.

Yours ever
Niels Bohr

# Honors and Prizes

The present survey of academic honors bestowed on Hevesy only lists data which have been confirmed either by the respective institutions or by means of original scrolls and documents in the hands of the Hevesy family. The survey thus supersedes the tables published in "Memoirs of Fellows of the Royal Society", in several International Biographical Dictionaries, as well as in articles about Hevesy written on various occasions: all these sources contain erroneous and discrepant information.

Membership of local associations and societies representing different branches of the sciences, biology, and medicine in many European and American universities are not included.

It has not been possible to obtain confirmation of all the academic honors mentioned by one source or the other. These unconfirmed data are listed separately. Readers of this biography are invited to provide additional information or documentation on this matter.

## Honorary Degrees

| University of | Year |
| --- | --- |
| Cape Town, South Africa | 1929 |
| Budapest, Hungary | 1945 |
| Uppsala, Sweden | 1945 |
| Copenhagen, Denmark | 1950 |
| São Paulo, Brazil | 1954 |
| Rio de Janeiro, Brazil | 1955 |
| Torino, Italy | 1957 |
| Vermont, USA | 1958 |

| | |
|---|---|
| Freiburg i.Br., Germany | 1958 |
| Liège, Belgium | 1959 |
| London, Great Britain | 1960 |
| Cambridge, Great Britain | 1964 |
| Budapest, Hungary (Engineering) | 1965 |

## Prizes

| | |
|---|---|
| Canizzaro Prize (Acad. Rome) | 1929 |
| Nobel Prize (Acad. Stockholm) | 1943 |
| Copley medal (Royal Society, London) | 1949 |
| Faraday medal (Chemical Society, Britain) | 1950 |
| Bailey medal (Roy. Coll. Physicians, London) | 1951 |
| Silvanus Thompson medal (Brit. Soc. Radiology, London) | 1956 |
| Medal of the City of Paris | 1957 |
| Medal Chemical Society of Japan | 1958 |
| Cothenius medal, Akademie d. Naturforscher (Halle) | 1959 |
| Atoms for Peace Award (New York, USA) | 1959 |
| Rosenberger medal (Chicago, USA) | 1961 |
| Niels Bohr medal (Copenhagen) | 1961 |
| George Washington Award (Am.-Hung. Studies Found. USA) | 1966 |

## Membership of Academies and Learned Societies

| | |
|---|---|
| Danish Academy, Copenhagen, Denmark | 1925 |
| Academy of Heidelberg, Germany | 1926 |
| Academy of Gothenburg, Sweden | 1931/45* |
| Royal Society, London, Great Britain | 1939 |
| Swedish Academy, Stockholm, Sweden | 1942/51* |
| Hungarian Academy, Budapest, Hungary | 1945 |
| Royal Institution, London, Great Britain | 1947 |
| Acad. Lincei, Rome, Italy | 1947 |
| American Academy Arts and Sciences, USA | 1950 |

| | |
|---|---|
| Academy in Bruxelles, Belgium | 1950 |
| Indian Academy of Science, India | 1950 |
| Bunsen Gesellschaft, Germany | 1951 |
| American Soc. European Chemists and Pharmacist, USA | 1951 |
| Order pour le Mérite, Bonn, Germany | 1957 |
| Chemical Society of Japan | 1958 |
| British Inst. Radiology and Röntgen Society, London | 1958 |
| American Soc. Nuclear Medicine | 1959 |
| Akademie d. Naturforscher, Leopoldine, Halle, Germany | 1959 |
| Pontifical Academy of Science, Rome, Italy | 1961 |
| World Academy of Arts and Sciences | 1962 |
| Soc. Nuclear Medicine, Europe | 1964 |
| Internat. Academy of Astronautics, Paris, France | 1965 |
| Academy of Vienna, Austria | 1965 |

*\* foreign member/Swedish member.*


Danish Cancer Research Prize: ⎫
Copernicus Prize, Königsberg: ⎬ not confirmed
dr.h.c., University of Ghent: ⎭

Unio Internationalis contra Cancrum: date and occasion unknown.

# Index of Names

Aston, F. W., British chemist,
1877-1945
atomic nucleus, isotopes

Auer v. Welshbach, C., Austrian
chemist 1858-1929
rare earth elements, Auer lighter

Baxter, G. P., American chemist
1876-1953
atomic weight determinations

Brønsted, J. N., Danish chemist
1879-1947, reaction kinetics,
isotope separation

Bohr, Niels, Danish physicist,
1885-1962
atomic model, quantum theory,
complementarity

Chadwick, J., British physicist
1891-1974
discoverer of neutron

Chievitz, O., Danish physician,
1883-1946

Christiansen, J. A., Danish chemist, 1888-1969
chemical reactions, kinetics

Cockcroft, J. D., British physicist,
1897-1967
accelerators, atomic energy

Coster, D., Dutch physicist,
1889-1950
co-discoverer of Hafnium

Darwin, C. G., British physicist,
1887-1963

Egerton, A. C. G., British physicist, 1886-1959

Einstein, A., German born physicist, 1879-1955
relativity

Euler, H. v., Swedish chemist,
1873-1964
enzymes, radiobiology

Fajans, K., Polish born physical
chemist, 1887-1975
radioactivity

Fermi, E., Italian born physicist,
1901-1954
induced radioactivity, chain
reaction

Franck, J., German born physicist,
1882-1964
atomic physics, photosynthesis

Frisch, O. R., Austrian born
physicist, 1904-1979
nuclear physics

Geiger, H., German physicist,
1882-1945
radioactivity, Geiger-counter

Gróh, G., Hungarian chemist,
1886-1952

Goldschmidt, V. M., Swiss born
mineralogist, 1888-1947
geochemistry

Haber, F., German chemist,
1868-1934
synthesis of ammonia

Hahn, O., German physicist,
1879-1968 radioactivity,
nuclear fission

Hansen, H. M., Danish physicist,
1886-1956

Hönigschmid, O., German chemist,
1878-1945
atomic weight determinations

Huggins, Ch., American physician,
1901-
cancer research

Jacobsen, J. C., Danish physicist,
1895-1965

Joliot-Curie, I., (1897-1956) and
F., (1900-1958), French physicists
induced radioactivity

Kamen, M. D., American chemist
1913-
radio-carbon

Klein, O., Swedish physicist,
1894-1977
Klein-Nishina formula

Kramers, H. A., Dutch physicist,
1894-1952

Krogh, A., Danish physiologist,
1874-1947
capillary system, isotopes in
biology

Lawrence, E., American physicist, 1901-1958
cyclotron

Lawson, R., British physicist, 1890-1960

Lockner, D., Swedish hematologist, 1928-

Lomholt, S., Danish dermatologist, 1888-1949

Lorentz, H. A., Dutch physicist, 1853-1928

Lorenz, R., Austrian chemist, 1863-1929

Mach, E., Austrian physicist and philosopher, 1838-1916

Meitner, L., Austrian physicist, 1878-1968
radioactivity, nuclear fission

Meyer, G., German chemist
Professor in Freiburg

Meyer, St., Austrian physicist, 1872-1949
radioactivity, Vienna Radium Institute

Meyerhof, O., German physiologist, 1884-1951
muscle physiology

Moseley, H. G. J., British physicist, 1887-1915
X-ray spectroscopy, isotopy

Needham, J., British biochemist, 1900-

Nernst, W., German physical-chemist, 1864-1941
thermodynamics

Nishina, Y., Japanese physicist, 1890-1951
hafnium, rare earths, nuclear physics

Paneth, F. A., Austrian born chemist 1887-1958
radioactive indicators, meteorites

Parnas, J. K., Polish chemist, 1884-1949
metabolism

Planck, M., German physicist, 1858-1947
quantum of action

Polanyi, M., Hungarian physicist-philosopher, 1891-1976

Rehberg, P. B., Danish physiologist,
1895-

Rolla, L., Italian chemist
1889-1960
rare earth elements

Rosseland, S., Norwegian physicist,
1894-1985

Rubens, H., German physicist,
1865-1922
radiation

Rubinowicz, A., Polish physicist,
1889-1974

Rutherford, E., New-Zealand born
British physicist,
1871-1937
radioactivity, atomic nucleus

Schönheimer, R., German born
biochemist,
1898-1941
heavy isotopes in biochemistry

Scott, A., British chemist,
1853-1947
element 72

Siegbahn, M., Swedish physicist,
1886-1951
X-ray spectroscopy

Solvay, E., Belgian chemist,
1838-1922
founder of conseil Solvay - conferences

Urbain, G., French chemist,
1871-1938
rare earth elements, "celtium"

Urey, H., American physicist,
1893-1980
separation of "heavy" isotopes

Ussing, H. H., Danish physiologist and biochemist, 1911-
permeability, ion transport

Willstätter, R., German chemist,
1872-1942
chlorophyll, photosynthesis

Wilson, C. T. R., British physicist,
1869-1959
cloud chamber

# Glossary

*Curie* The Curie is a measuring unit for the quantity of a radioactive substance. Originally it was the equivalent of 1 gram of radium which decays at a rate of $3.7 \cdot 10^9$ disintegrating atoms per second. Now it applies to any radioactive isotope and denotes the quantity which disintegrates by emission of the same amount of radiation, namely $3.7 \cdot 10^9$ disintegrations per second (abbr. Ci.). One milliCurie is one thousandth, and one microCurie is one millionth of this quantity (abbr., mCi or μCi.).

*Cyclotron* is a machine, first built by E. Lawrence at the University of California, with which to accelerate subatomic particles – and also hydrogen atoms – to very high speeds. When stable elements are bombarded with these high speed (high energy) particles, radioactive elements (radioisotopes) are formed.

*Decay period* or *half-life* are the terms which denote how fast radioactive elements are transformed into their "daughter" products. The term half-life is used most frequently and denotes the time it takes until half of all atoms present in a sample at any given time have been transformed. The half-life of radium is c. 1600 years, that of radon (cf."r") is c. 4 days, and that of artificially produced radio-phosphorus is c. 14.5 days.

*Electroscope* is an instrument used at the beginning of this century for the detection and measurement of ionizing radiation (cf."r"). Two thin metal foils are fastened to an insulating rod. The foils repulse each other when electrically charged. Ionizing radiation reduces the charge and causes the foils to collapse. The time required for the foils to fall back after having been charged is a measure of the radiation present.

*Geiger-Müller counter* is a detector of ionizing radiation (cf. "r") invented in 1912. It is based on the fact that the electrical potential between two electrodes in a chamber will decrease when ionizing radiation passes through the chamber. This "pulse" is amplified and registered. The number of pulses per time unit is a measure of the radiation present.

*Isotope* from the Greek "iso-topos" "is the same place" is the term describing varieties of atoms which have identical chemical properties and therefore occupy the same place in the periodic table (cf. "p"); but they differ in atomic weight. Isotopes of stable elements are sometimes called "light" or "heavy", for example heavy hydrogen or heavy water, while radioactive isotopes are always denoted by the sum of the elementary particles (protons and neutrons) contained in the nucleus. This sum determines their atomic weight: for example phosphorus-32 or carbon-14.

*Neutron* is an electrically neutral elementary particle with a mass equal to one (relative to hydrogen) discovered by the British physicist J. Chadwick in 1932. Neutrons are produced for example when metallic beryllium is bombarded with alpha particles from radium.

*Neutron sources:* the most frequently used source for neutrons until the 1940ies was a mixture of metallic beryllium powder either with radon gas (cf. "r") or with radium salt enclosed in an ampulla. A radon-beryllium source lasts only a short time because radon has a half-life of c. 4 days; a radium-beryllium source, however, lasts a long time (half-life 1600 years). Since the late 1940ies nuclear reactors are the predominant and most powerful neutron sources available.

*Periodic table (system)* If all stable elements occurring in Nature are listed in the order of their atomic weights – as Mendelejev did around 1860 – similar properties of the elements appear periodically. This periodic chemical similarity could be explained on the basis of Bohr's theory of atomic constitution.

*Pitchblende* is a metallic looking mineral containing both radium and uranium. It was found in Joachimsthal (Czechoslovakia) and was used by Mme. Curie, Rutherford, and others to prepare the naturally occurring radioactive elements in a pure form.

*Radiation (ionizing radiation)* is the term used both for the particles and the electro-magnetic waves emitted by naturally occurring or by artificially produced radioactive elements. Alpha rays consist of helium atoms, beta rays of electrons, gamma rays are electro-magnetic waves. Also X-rays, discovered by Röntgen, are ionizing radiation. The term gamma rays is used if the radiation is emitted by a radioactive element, X-rays denote the radiation produced for example in a Röntgen tube.

*Radioactivity* discovered by the French scientist A. H. Becquerel (1896) is the term for the spontaneous emission of subatomic particles (alpha and beta particles) and of electromagnetic waves (gamma rays) by some elements occurring in Nature, such as radium, uranium, polonium, and others.

*Radio-phosphorus* is formed when sulphur is bombarded with neutrons. Hevesy placed carbon disulphide (a liquid) into a 2 liter flask and the neutron source in its center. After about 2 weeks, he extracted the phosphorus-32 formed using a chemical procedure.

*Radium* is a radioactive element found in Nature, which spontaneously disintegrates into a gaseous element called radon or radium emanation. Radon exists only for a short time and disintegrates into a solid element radium A (abbr. RaA). The process of further disintegration continues through RaD, RaE and RaF. The end product of this series is ordinary lead. RaD is an isotope of lead, RaE is an isotope of bismuth, and RaF is an isotope of polonium.

*Spectroscopy* denotes the study of radiation by dispersing its components according to wave-length (frequency). In *light spectroscopy* the radiation from any source of light such as the sun or a glowing substance is dispersed in a prism or an optical grid. The resulting "spectrum" is characteristic of the atomic structure of the light-emitter. In *X-ray spectroscopy* the prism is replaced by a diffracting crystal. Moseley found a relationship between the frequency of the X-ray emission and the atomic number of the element forming the crystal.

*Mass spectrometer* is an instrument by which one can determine atomic mass. If a stream of ions passes through a strong magnetic field, the ions are deflected and the degree of deflection is a measure of their mass. Different isotopes of any given element will thus be separated from each other according to their masses. In this way the number of isotopes as well as their relative abundance can be determined.

*Wilson cloud chamber* is a detector of ionizing radiation; it consists of a chamber in which air is expanded to form "fog". Radiation passing the chamber causes the "fog" to condense into droplets, and hence to form a "track" which can be viewed (photographed) through the transparent wall of the chamber.

# Bibliography*)


1) Über die schmelzelektrolytische Abscheidung der Alkalimetalle aus Aetzalkalien und die Löslichkeit dieser Metalle in der Schmelze, Dissertation (Freiburg, 1908)
2) Über die schmelzelektrolytische Abscheidung der Alkalimetalle aus Aetzalkalien, Z. Elektrochem. **15** (1909) 529
3) R. Lorenz und --, Widerstandsöfen mit elektrisch geheiztem Nickeldraht, Z. Elektrochem. **16** (1910) 185
4) Über die Elektrolyse in Pyridin gelöster Erdalkalijodide, Z. Elektrochem. **16** (1910) 672
5) Über die elektrolytische Darstellung des Rubidiums, Z. anorg. Chem. **67** (1910) 242
6) Über Alkalihydroxyde I., Z. phys. Chem. **73** (1910) 667
7) -- und R. Lorenz, Das kapillarelektrische Phänomen im Schmelzfluss, Z. phys. Chem. **74** (1910) 443
8) -- und E. Wolff, Über das Silver-Nickel Thermoelement, Phys. Z. **11** (1910) 473
9) Über den Nachweis der Aktiniumemanation in aktiniumhaltigen Mineralien, Phys. Z. **12** (1911) 1213
10) Über die Löslichkeit von Aktiniumemanation in Flüssigkeiten und Kohle, Phys. Z. **12** (1911) 1214
11) R. Lorenz, --, und E. Wolff, Beiträge zur Kenntnis der Natur der Metallnebel in Schmelzflüssen, Z. phys. Chem. **76** (1911) 732
12) On the solubility of actinium emanation in liquids and in charcoal, J. Phys. Chem. **16** (1912) 429
13) The electrochemistry of radioactive bodies, Phil. Mag. **23** (1912) 628
14) Über den Zusammenhang zwischen den chemischen Eigenschaften der Radioelemente und der Reihenfolge radioaktiver Umwandlungen, Phys. Z. **13** (912) 672
15) Radioaktive Methoden in der Elektrochemie. (Bunsen-Vortrag), Z. Elektrochem. **18** (1912) 546; Phys. Z. **13** (1912) 715
16) The detection of actinium emanation in solutions of minerals, J. Phys. Chem. **16** (1912) 451
17) -- und R. E. Slade, Das elektrochemische Verhalten des Tantals, Z. Elektrochem. **18** (1912) 1001
18) Die Valenz der Radioelemente, Phys. Z. **14** (1913) 49
19) -- und L. v. Putnoky, Über die Diffusion des Urans, Phys. Z. **14** (1913) 63
20) Diffusion und Valenz der Radioelemente, Phys. Z. **14** (1913) 1202
21) The valency of the radioelements, Phil. Mag. **25** (1913) 390
22) Die Eigenschaften der Emanationen, Jahrb. Radioaktivität und Elektronik **10** (1913) 198
23) Die Spannungsreihe der Radioelemente, Z. Elektrochem. **19** (1913) 291
24) Radio-active elements as indicators in chemistry and physics, British Association (1913)
25) -- und Fritz Paneth, Die Löslichkeit des Bleisulfids und Bleichromats, Z. anorg. Chem. **82** (1913) 323
26) The diffusion of uranium, Phil. Mag. **25** (1913) 415
27) -- und Fritz Paneth, RaD als "Indikator" des Bleis, Z. anorg. Chem. **82** (1913) 322
28) F. Paneth und --, Über Versuche zur Trennung des Radium D von Blei, Mitt. Inst. Radiumforsch. Wien (1913) No. 42


*) From: Nuclear Physics 1967, vol. A 98, p.12.

29) Fritz Paneth und – –, Über Radioelemente als Indikatoren in der analytischen Chemie, Mitt. Inst. Radiumforsch. Wien (1913) No. 43

30) F. Paneth und – –, Über die elektrochemische Vertretbarkeit von Radioelementen, Mitt. Inst. Radiumforsch. Wien (1913) No. 44

31) F. Paneth und – –, Über die Gewinnung von Polonium, Mitt. Inst. Radiumforsch. Wien (1913) No. 45

32) The diffusion and valency of the radio-elements, Phil. Mag. **27** (1914) 586

33) Bericht über die Verhandlungen der British Association in Birmingham, Z. Elektrochem. **20** (1914) 88

34) – – und F. Paneth, Zur Elektrochemie des Poloniums, Monatshefte für Chemie (1915) No. 36; Mitt. Inst. Radiumforsch. Wien (1914) No. 47

35) – – und F. Paneth, Über die Darstellung von Radium D in sichtbaren Mengen und seine chemische Identität mit Blei, Ber. Dt. Chem. Ges. **47** (1914) 2784

36) – – und F. Paneth, Zur Frage der isotopen Elemente, Mitt. Inst. Radiumforsch. Wien (1914) No. 66; Phys. Z. **15** (1914) 797

37) Über die Grösse und Beweglichkeit der Elektrizitätsträger in Flüssigkeiten. Erster Teil, Jahrb. Radioaktivität und Elektronik **11** (1914) 419. Zweiter Teil, Ibid. **13** (1916) 271

38) – – und F. Paneth, Zur Frage der isotopen Elemente (Erwiderung auf die gleichnamige Abhandlung von K. Fajans), Phys. Z. **16** (1915) 45

39) Über den Austausch der Atome zwischen festen und flüssigen Phasen, Phys. Z. **16** (1915) 52; Mitt. Inst. Radiumforsch. Wien (1915) No. 75; Mh. Chem. (1915) No. 36

40) – – und F. Paneth, Über galvanische Ketten aus Blei-Isotopen, Mh. Chem. (1915) No. 36; Mitt. Inst. Radiumforsch. Wien (1915) No. 76

41) – – und Elisabeth Róna, Die Lösungsgeschwindigkeit molekularer Schichten, Z. phys. Chem. **89** (1915) 294

42) – – und F. Paneth, Zur Frage der isotopen Elemente, Phys. Z. **17** (1916) 4

43) Über die Ladung und Grösse von Ionen und Dispersoiden, Kolloid Z. **21** (1917) 129

44) Die Leitfähigkeit der Dispersoide, Kolloid Z. **21** (1917) 136

45) Über elektrolytische und kolloide Lösungen von Radioelementen, Mitt. Inst. Radiumforsch. Wien (1918) No. 115

46) Elektrolyse und elektrolytische Polarisation, Handb. Elektr. und Magnetismus **2** (1919) 473

47) Die Platzwechselgeschwindigkeit der Ionen im Kristall, Z. Phys. **2** (1920) 148

48) Elektrizitätsleitung und Diffusion in festen Salzen, Mitt. Inst. Radiumforsch. Wien (1920) No. 132

49) – – und L. Zechmeister, Über den intermolekularen Platzwechsel gleichartiger Atome, Ber. Dt. Chem. Ges. **53** (1920) 410

50) – – und L. Zechmeister, Über den Verlauf des Umwandlungsvorgangs isomerer Ionen, Z. Elektrochem. **26** (1920) 151

51) J. N. Brønsted and – –, The separation of the isotopes of mercury, Nature **106** (1920) 144

52) Die Selbstdiffusion in geschmolzenem Blei, Z. Elektrochem. **26** (1920) 363

53) J. Gróh und – –, Die Selbstdiffusionsgeschwindigkeit des geschmolzenen Bleis, Ann. der Phys. **63** (1920) 85

54) Über die Unterscheidung zwischen elektrolytischer und metallischer Stromleitung in festen und geschmolzenen Verbindungen, Mat. Fys. Medd. Dan. Vid. Selsk. **3** (1921) No. 12

55) Über den Zusammenhang zwischen Siedepunkt und Leitfähigkeit elektrolytisch leitender Flüssigkeiten, Mat. Fys. Medd. Dan. Vid. Selsk. **3** (1921) No. 13

56) Die Beweglichkeit der Ionen, die dem Lösungsmittel eigen sind, Z. Elektrochem. **27** (1921) 21

57) J. N. Brønsted and – –, The separation of the isotopes of chlorine, Nature **107** (1921) 619

58) J. N. Brønsted und – –, Über die Trennung der Isotopen des Quecksilbers, Z. phys. Chem. **99** (1921) 189

59) J. Gróh und – –, die Selbstdiffusionsgeschwindigkeit in festem Blei, Ann. der Phys. **65** (1921) 216

60) Notiz über die Beweglichkeit einwertiger organischer Ionen, Z. Elektrochem. **27** (1921) 77

61) Über Materietransport im Kristall und Kristallit, Z. Phys. **10** (1922) 80

62) J. N. Brønsted and – –, The atomic weight of mercury from different sources, Nature **109** (1922) 780

63) An attempt to influence the rate of radioactive disintegration by use of penetrating radiation, Nature **110** (1922) 216

64) Über den Zusammenhang zwischen Elektrizitätsleitung und Wärmeleitung in elektrolytisch leitenden Kristallen, Z. Phys. **10** (1922) 84

65) Über die Auflockerung von Kristallgittern, Z. phys. Chem. **101** (1922) 337

66) Über die Trennung von Isotopen, Oesterr. Chemiker-Ztg. **25** (1922) 80

67) J. N. Brønsted and – –, The separation of the isotopes of mercury, Phil. Mag. **43** (1922) 31

68) Über die Auffindung des Hafniums und den gegenwärtigen Stand unserer Kenntnisse von diesem Element, Ber. Dt. Chem. Ges. **56** (1923) 1503; Chemiker-Ztg. **47** (1923) 345

69) Note on the chemistry of hafnium, Chem. News **127** (1923) 33

70) On the new element hafnium, Chemy. Ind. **42** (1923) 258

71) Hafnium – a new element, Raw Materials Rev. **2** (1923) 133

72) D. Coster and – –, On the missing element of atomic number 72, Nature **111** (1923) 79

73) D. Coster and – –, On the new element hafnium, Nature **111** (1923) 182 and 252

74) On the chemistry of hafnium, Chemy. Ind. **42** (1923) 929

75) D. Coster and – –, Über das Element der Atomzahl 72, Naturw. **11** (1923) 133

76) Jordens alder, Medd. fra Dansk Geol. Forening (1923) p. 13

77) – – and V. Thal Jantzen, The separation of hafnium from zirconium, Chem. News **127** (1923) 353

78) Bohrsche Theorie und Radioaktivität, Naturw. **11** (1923) 604

79) Über das neue Element Hafnium, Oesterr. Chemiker-Z. **26** (1923) 118

80) D. Coster and – –, On celtium and hafnium, Nature **111** (1923) 462

81) The absorption and translocation of lead by plants, Biochem. J. **17** (1923) 439; Nature **112** (1923) 772 (abstract)

82) – – und Fritz Paneth, Lehrbuch der Radioaktivität. (Joh. Ambr. Barth, Leipzig, 1923). Zweite, völlig umgearb. Aufl. (Leipzig, 1931).
A Manual of Radioactivity. Oxford Univ. Press (1926); Second revised ed. (Oxford, 1938).
Theory of Radioactivity, Scientific Thinking, Berlin 1924 and Leningrad 1925 (in Russian)

83) – – and Valdemar Thal Jantzen, The hafnium content of zirconium ores, J. Chem. Soc. **123** (1923) 3218; Chem. News **128** (1924) 78 and 341

84) – – and V. Berglund, Zircon and hafnium oxides, Chem. News (1924) December

85) The hafnium content of some historical zirconium preparations, Nature **113** (1924) 384

86) – – and Viggo Berglund, The density of the oxides of zirconium and hafnium, J. Chem. Soc. **125** (1924) 2372

87) – – and V. Thal Jantzen, Der Hafniumgehalt von Zirkonmineralen, I. Z. anorg. allg. Chem. **133** (1924) 113; II. Ibid. **136** (1924) 387

88) – – und V. Thal Jantzen, Über den Hafniumgehalt einiger historischer Zirkonpräparate, Naturw. **12** (1924) 729

89) Christiansen, J.-A., – – and S. Lomholt, Recherches, par une méthode radiochimique, sur la circulation du bismuth dans l'organisme, C.R. **178** (1924) 1324

90) Christiansen, J.-A., – – and Sv. Lomholt, Recherches par une méthode radiochimique, sur la circulation du plomb dans l'organisme, C. R. **179** (1924) 291

91) – –, J. A. Christiansen and V. Berglund, Die Löslichkeit der Doppelfluoride des Zirkons und Hafniums, Z. anorg. und allg. Chem. **144** (1925) 69

92) – – and K. Kimura, The solubilities of the phosphates of zirconium and hafnium, J. Amer. Chem. Soc. **47** (1925) 2540

93) – – und E. Madsen, Über die Trennung des Hafniums von Zirkon, Z. angew. Chem. **38** (1925) 228

94) – – and V. Berglund, Zircon and hafnium oxides, J. Chem. Soc. (1925) November

95) The discovery and properties of hafnium, Chem. Revs. **2** (1925) 1

96) Recherches sur les propriétés du hafnium, Mat. Fys. Medd. Dan. Vid. Selsk. **6** (1925) No. 7

97) Investigations on the properties of hafnium, Mat. Fys. Medd. Dan. Vid. Selsk. **7** (1925) No. 8

98) – – and K. Kimura, Über die Phosphate des Zirkons und Hafniums, Z. angew. Chem., **38** (1925) 774

99) Über Gesetzmässigkeiten innerhalb der seltenen Erden und der Titangruppe, Z. anorg. allg. Chem. **147** (1925) 217

Nachtrag zu der Mitteilung „Über Gesetzmässigkeiten innerhalb der seltenen Erden", Ibid. **150** (1925) 1

100) The atomic weights of zirconium and hafnium, Nature **115** (1925) 335

101) – – and A. Obrutsheva, Self-diffusion in solid metals, Nature **115** (1925) 674

102) Über die Anwendung von radioaktiven Indikatoren in der Biologie, Biochem. Z. **173** (1926) 175

103) On the missing element 87, Mat. Fys. Medd. Dan. Vid. Selsk. **7** (1926) No. 11

104) Über die elektrische Leitfähigkeit im Einkristall und in Kristallaggregaten, Z. Phys. **36** (1926) 481

105) Hafnium. Handb. Mineralchem., **3** (1926) 1170

106) – – und M. Lögstrup, Über das Acetylacetonat des Zirkoniums und des Hafniums, Ber. Dt. Chem. Ges. **59** (1926) 1890

107) The use of X-rays for the discovery of new elements, Chem. Revs. **3** (1927) 321

108) Das Element Hafnium (Springer, Berlin 1927)

109) The radioactivity of potassium, Nature **120** (1927) 838

110) Über Zinkblende, Wurtzitgitter und Ionengitter, Z. phys. Chem. **127** (1927) 401

111) Die seltenen Erden vom Standpunkte des Atombaus (Bd. 5: Struktur der Materie; Springer, Berlin 1927)

112) – – und J. Böhm, Die quantitative Bestimmung des Tantals auf röntgenspektroskopischem Wege, Z. anorg. allg. Chem. **164** (1927) 69

113) – – und G. Rienäcker, Über die Auflockerung der Kristallgitter, Ann. der Phys. **84** (1927) 674

114) Die elektrische Leitfähigkeit als Kriterium der Bindungsart, Z. Elektrochem. **34** (1928) 463

115) – – und M. Lögstrup, Die Trennung der Isotope des Kaliums, Z. anorg. allg. Chem. **171** (1928) 1

116) – – und Otto Stern, Fritz Habers Arbeiten auf dem Gebiete der physikalischen Chemie und Elektrochemie, Naturw. **16** (1928) 1062

117) – – und K. Würstlin, Über das Häufigkeitsverhältnis Zirkonium/Hafnium und Niob/Tantal, Z. phys. Chem. **139**, Abt. A. (1928) 605

118) Quantitative chemical analysis by X-rays and its application, Nature **124** (1929) 841

119) Freiherr Carl Auer von Welsbach, Akad. Mitt. Freiburg **4** (1929) 17

120) Das Alter der Grundstoffe, Vortrag in der Freiburger Wissensch. Ges. (1929) Heft 17

121) – – und W. Seith, Über die Platzwechselgeschwindigkeit des Silbers im Silbertellurid-Antimonid und -Zinnid, Z. anorg. allg. Chem. **180** (1929) 150

122) – – und M. Biltz. Kinetische Vorgänge an metallischen Oberflächen, Z. phys. Chem. Abt. B **3** (1929) 271

123) – –, E. Alexander und K. Würstlin, Über das Häufigkeitsverhältnis Niob-Tantal in Titan-mineralien, Z. anorg. allg. Chem. **181** (1929) 95

124) – – und W. Seith, Der radioaktive Rückstoss im Dienste von Diffusionsmessungen, Z. Phys. **56** (1929) 790; Berichtigung, Ibid. **56** (1929) 869

125) J. N. Brønsted and – –, On the separation of isotopes, Phil. Mag. **7** (1929) 631

126) Die seltenen Erden im Lichte des atomtheoretisch begründeten periodischen Systems, Scientia **47** (1930) 245

127) Quantitative Spektralanalyse mit Röntgenstrahlen, Metallwirt. **9** (1930) 801

128) Über Verteilung der schweren Metalle im Organismus, Forsch. Fortschr. **6** (1930) 253

129) Richard Lorenz. Erinnerungen aus den Züricher Jahren, Helv. Chim. Acta **13** (1930) 13

130) The age of the earth, Science **77** (1930) 509

131) – – and A. Guenther, Search for an inactive isotope of the element 84 (Polonium), Nature **125** (1930) 744

132) Quantitative analysis by X-rays, Nature **125** (1930) 776

133) Über den Zusammenhang zwischen Ladung und Grösse der Ionen, Z. phys. Chem. A **149** (1930) 472

134) – – und E. Löwenstein, Über Subhaloide der Homologen des Quecksilbers, Z. anorg. allg. Chem. **187** (1930) 266

135) Quantitative spectral analysis by X-rays, J. scient Instr. **7** (1930) 296

136) – – und O. H. Wagner, Die Löslichkeit der Halogenide des Zirkoniums und Hafniums, Z. anorg. allg. Chem. **191** (1930) 194

137) – – und A. Guenther, Versuche, ein stabiles Isotop des Poloniums aufzufinden, Z. anorg. allg. Chem. **194** (1930) 162

138) Mikroanalyse auf röntgenspektroskopischem Wege. Festschrift für Friedrich Emich, Mikrochemie **163** (1930)

139) – –, E. Alexander und K. Würstlin, Die Häufigkeit der Elemente der Vanadiumgruppe in Eruptivgesteinen, Z. anorg. allg. Chem. **194** (1930) 316

140) – –, J. Böhm und A. Faessler, Quantitative röntgenspektroskopische Analyse mit Sekundärstrahlen, Z. Phys. **63** (1930) 74

141) – – und J. C. Calvert, Quantitative Bestimmung von Kalium in Bodenproben auf röntgenspektroskopischem Wege, Naturw. **18** (1930) 529

142) – – und O. H. Wagner, Die Verteilung des Thoriums im tierischen Organismus, Arch. exp. Path. Pharmak. **149** (1930) 336

143) Quantitative röntgenspektroskopische Analyse mit Sekundärstrahlen, Ergebn. d. techn. Röntgenkunde **2** (1931) 262

144) The chemistry and geochemistry of the titanium group. (Hugo Müller Lecture), J. Chem. Soc., (1931) January

145) – – und E. Alexander, Fluoreszenzausbeute im L-Gebiet, Naturw. **19** (1931) 825

146) – – und Erika Cremer, Über die Sulfate des Zirkoniums und Hafniums, Z. anorg. allg. Chem. **195** (1931) 339

147) – – und W. Seith, Diffusion in Metallen, Z. Elektrochem. **37** (1931) 528

148) – –, R. Hobbie and A. Holmes, Lead content of rocks, Nature **128** (1931) 1038

149) – –, W. Seith und M. Pahl, Über die Radioaktivität des Kaliums (Bodenstein Festband), Z. phys. Chem. Ergänzungsbd. (1931) 309

150) Anwendung radiochemischer Methoden, Forsch. Fortschr. **8** (1932) 258

151) Die geochemische und kosmische Häufigkeit des Bleis, Fortschr. Miner., Kristallogr., Petrogr. **16** (1932) 147

152) Radiochemische Methoden in Chemie, Physik und Biologie, Z. Elektrochem. **38** (1932) 504

153) Chemical analysis by X-rays and its application, The George Fisher Baker-Non-President Lectureship in Chemistry at Cornell University (Mc Graw-Hill Book Comp., Inc., New York 1932)

154) – – and E. Alexander, Intensity ratio of fluorescent X-ray lines, Nature **129** (1932) 315

155) – – und E. Alexander, Intensitätsverhältnisse im L-Gebiet der seltenen Erden, Z. Phys. **78** (1932) 576

156) – – und R. Hobbie, Über die Ermittlung des Bleigehaltes von Gesteinen, Z. analyt. Chem. **88** (1932) 1

157) – – und R. Hobbie, Über die Existenz des Elementes 85, Z. anorg. allg. Chem. **208** (1932) 107

158) – – und M. Pahl, Radioactivity of samarium, Nature **130** (1932) 846

159) – –, W. Seith und A. Keil, Die Auflockerungswärme des Bleigitters, Z. Phys. **79** (1932) 197

160) Diffusion in Kristallen, Naturw. **21** (1933) 357

161) Materietransport in festen Körpern, Z. Elektrochem. **39** (1933) 490

162) Chemie der Meteoriten und Folgerungen für den Aufbau der Erde, Handb. Geophysik **2** (1933) 1090

163) Frederick Soddy, The interpretation of the atom (Review), Nature **131** (1933) 4

164) – – and M. Pahl, Range of radiation from samarium, Nature **131** (1933) 434

165) F. W. Aston, Mass-spectra and isotopes (Review), Nature **132** (1933) 983

166) – – und E. Alexander, Praktikum der chemischen Analyse mit Röntgenstrahlen (Akad. Verlags-Ges., Leipzig 1933)

167) – – und R. Hobbie, Die Ermittlung des Molybdän- und Wolframgehaltes von Gesteinen, Z. anorg. allg. Chem. **212** (1933) 134

168) – –, M. Pahl und R. Hosemann, Die Radioaktivität des Samariums, Z. Phys. **83** (1933) 43

169) – – und K. Würstlin, Die Häufigkeit des Zirkoniums, Z. anorg. allg. Chem. **216** (1934) 305

170) – – und K. Würstlin, Über die Häufigkeit des Strontiums, Z. anorg. allg. Chem. **216** (1934) 312

171) – –, A. Merkel und K. Würstlin, Die Häufigkeit des Chroms und Mangans, Z. anorg. allg. Chem. **219** (1934) 192

172) – – und M. Pahl, Über die Radioaktivität von seltenen Erden, Z. phys. Chem. **A169** (1934) 147

173) – – und W. Dullenkopf, Über das Tetrafluorid des Zirkons und Hafniums, Z. anorg. allg. Chem. **221** (1934) 161

174) – – und W. Dullenkopf, Zur Frage des Umwandlungsproduktes des Kaliums, Z. anorg. allg. Chem. **221** (1934) 167

175) – – and E. Hofer, Diplogen and fish, Nature **133** (1934) 495

176) – – und A. Faessler, Über die Wirkung von Kathodenstrahlen auf Gemische, Z. Phys. **88** (1934) 336

177) – – and H. Lay, Fluorescent yield of X-ray emission, Nature **134** (1934) 98

178) – – und E. Hofer, Die Verweilzeit des Wassers im menschlichen Körper, Klin. Wschr. **13** (1934) 1524

179) – –, M. Pahl and R. Hosemann, Radioactivity of potassium, Nature **134** (1934) 377

180) – – and E. Hofer, Elimination of water from the human body, Nature **134** (1934) 879

181) – – und T. Somiya, Über Platinschwarz, Z. phys. Chem. **A 171** (1934) 41

182) – – und E. Hofer, Der Austausch des Wassers im Fischkörper, Seylers Z. physiol. Chem. **225** (1934) 28

183) – – und W. Seith, Diffusion in Metallen, Metallwirt. **13** (1934) 479

184) Artificial radioactivity of scandium, Mat. Fys. Medd. Dan. Vid. Selsk. **13** (1935) No. 3

185) Die Radioaktivität des Kaliums, Naturw. **23** (1935) 583

186) Der schwere Wasserstoff in der Biologie, Naturw. **23** (1935) 775

187) Natural and artificial radioactivity of potassium, Nature **135** (1935) 96

188) – –, E. Hofer and A. Krogh, The permeability of the skin of frogs to water, as determined by $D_2O$ and $H_2O$, Scand. Arch. Physiol. **72** (1935) 199

189) – – and Hilde Levi, Radiopotassium and other artificial radio-elements, Nature **135** (1935) 580

190) – – and Hilde Levi, Artificial radioactivity of dysprosium and other rare earth elements, Nature **136** (1935) 103

191) O. Chievitz and – –, Radioactive indicators in the study of phosphorus metabolism in rats, Nature **136** (1935) 754

192) The discovery of hafnium, Current Science **5** (1936) 236

193) Isotopernes Anvendelse som Indikatorer i Kemi og Biologi, Naturens Verden **20** (1936) 289

194) Isotopernes Anvendelse i den kemiske Analyse, Naturens Verden **20** (1936) 357

195) Isotopernes Anvendelse til Undersøgelse af Stofskiftet i levende Organismer, Naturens Verden **20** (1936) 401

196) – –, K. Linderstrøm-Lang and C. Olsen, Atomic dynamics of plant growth, Nature **137** (1936) 66

197) O. R. Frisch, – – and H. A. C. McKay, Selective absorption of neutrons by gold, Nature **137** (1936) 149

198) – – and Hilde Levi, Action of slow neutrons on rare earth elements, Nature **137** (1936) 185

199) – – and Hilde Levi, The action of neutrons on the rare earth elements, Mat. Fys. Medd. Dan. Vid. Selsk **14** (1936) No. 5

200) – –, K. Linderstrøm-Lang and C. Olsen, Exchange of phosphorus atoms in plants and seeds, Nature **139** (1937) 149

201) O. Chievitz and – –, Studies on the metabolism of phosphorus in animals, Biol. Medd. Dan. Vid. Selsk. **13** (1937) No. 9

202) – – and E. Lundsgaard, Lecithinaemia following the administration of fat, Nature **140** (1937) 275

203) L. A. Hahn, – – and E C. Lundsgaard, The circulation of phosphorus in the body revealed by application of radioactive phosphorus as indicator, Biochem. J. **31** (1937) 1705

204) – –, J. Holst and A. Krogh, Investigations on the exchange of phosphorus in teeth using radioactive phosphorus as indicator, Biol. Medd. Dan. Vid. Selsk. **13** (1937) No. 13

205) – – K. Linderstrøm-Lang and N. Nielsen, Phosphorus exchange in yeast, Nature **140** (1937) 725

206) Tribute to the late Lord Rutherford. Nature, Suppl. **140** (1937) 1049

207) – – and F. A. Paneth, Radioelements as indicators in chemical and biological research, Sci. Progr. **32** (1937) 38

208) L. Hahn and – –, The formation of phosphatides in the brain tissue of adult animals, Scand. Arch. Physiol. **77** (1937) 148

209) L. Hahn and – –, Origin of yolk lecithin, Nature **140** (1937) 1059

210) L. Hahn and – –, Formation of phospatides in blood, C.R. Lab. Carlsberg, Sér. Chim. **22** (1938) 188

211) Self-diffusion in solids, Trans. Faraday Soc. **34** (1938) 841

212) Radioactive phosphorus as an indicator in biology, Nuovo Cimento **15** (1938) 279

213) The application of isotopic indicators in biological research, Enzymologia **5** (1938) 138

214) – –, T. Baranowski, A. J. Guthke, P. Ostern and J. Parnas, Untersuchungen über die Phosphor-übertragungen in der Glykolyse und Glykogenolyse, Acta Biol. Exp (Varsovie) **12** (1938) 34

215) – – and L. Hahn, Origin of phosphorus compounds in hens' eggs, Biol. Medd. Dan. Vid. Selsk. **14** (1938) No. 2

216) – – and H. Levi, Artificial activity of hafnium and some other elements, Mat. Fys. Medd. Dan. Vid. Selsk. **15** (1938) No. 11

217) L. A. Hahn and – –, Formation of phosphatides in liver perfusion experiments, Biochem. J. **32** (1938) 342

218) – – and O. Rebbe, Molecular "rejuvenation" of muscle tissue, Nature **141** (1938) 1097

219) A. H. W. Aten jun. and – –, Formation of milk, Nature **142** (1938) 111

220) – –, H. B. Levi and O. H. Rebbe, The origin of the phosphorus compounds in the embryo of the chicken, Biochem. J. **32** (1938) 2147

221) A. H. W. Aten jun. and – –, Diffusion of phosphate ions into blood corpuscles, Nature **142** (1938) 871

222) A. H. W. Aten jun. and – –, Fate of the sulphate radical in the animal body, Nature **142** (1938) 952

223) Blodlegemers Permeabilitet. Forhandl. ved. det 5. Nordiske Kemikermøde (København, Juli 1939)

224) Application of isotopes in biology, J. Chem. Soc. (1939) 1213

225) Le rôle des indicateurs isotopiques dans la recherche biologique, Acta Union Intern. contre le Cancer (Paris) **4** (1939) 175

226) – –, L. Hahn and O. Rebbe, Excretion of phosphorus, Biol. Medd. Dan. Vid. Selsk. **14** (1939) No. 3

227) – – and A. H. W. Aten jun., Interaction of plasma phosphate with the phosphorus compounds present in the corpuscles, Biol. Medd. Dan. Vid. Selsk. **14** (1939) No. 5

228) L. Hahn, – – and O. Rebbe, Permeability of corpuscles and muscle cells to potassium ions, Nature **143** (1939) 1021

229) L. Hahn and – –, Interaction between the phosphatides of the plasma and the corpuscles, Nature **144** (1939) 72

230) L. Hahn and – –, Phosphatide exchange between plasma and organs, Nature **144** (1939) 204

231) L. A. Hahn, – – and O. Rebbe, Do the potassium ions inside the muscle cells and blood corpuscles exchange with those present in the plasma? Biochem. J. **33** (1939) 1549

232) L. Hahn and – –, Formation of phosphatides in blood, C.R. Lab. Carlsberg, Sér. chim. **22** (1940) 188

233) Application of radioactive indicators in biology, Ann. Rev. Biochem. **9** (1940) 641

234) The use of radioactive isotopes of the common elements in physiology, Phys. Rev. **57** (1940) 240

235) – – and L. Hahn, Turnover of lecithin, cephalin and sphyngomyelin, Biol. Med. Dan. Vid Selsk. **15** (1940) No. 5

236) – – and L. Hahn, Rate of penetration of phosphatides through the capillary wall, Biol. Medd. Dan. Vid. Selsk. **15** (1940) No. 6

141

237) – – and L. Hahn, Rate of renewal of the acid soluble organic phosphorus compounds in the organs and the blood of the rabbit. With a note on the duration of life of the red blood corpuscles, Biol. Medd. Dan. Vid. Selsk. **15** (1940) No. 7

238) L. Hahn and – –, Turnover rate of nucleic acid, Nature **145** (1940) 549

239) – – and W. D. Armstrong, Exchange of radiophosphate by dental enamel. Proc. Amer. Soc. Biol. Chem., 34th Annual Meeting, Annex to J. Biol. Chem. **133** (1940) 14 (Abstract)

240) L. Hahn and – –, A method of blood volume determination, Acta Physiol. Scand. **1**, fasc. 1 (1940) 3

241) – – and C. F. Jacobsen, Rate of passage of water through capillary and cell walls, Acta Physiol. Scand. **1**, fasc. 1 (1940) 11

242) – –, H. B. Levi and O. H. Rebbe, Rate of rejuvenation of the skeleton, Biochem. J. **34** (1940) 532

243) – – and O. Rebbe, Rate of penetration of phosphate into muscle cells, Acta Physiol. Scand. **1**, fasc. 2 (1940) 171

244) – –, K. Linderstrøm-Lang, A. S. Keston and C. Olsen, Exchange of nitrogen atoms in the leaves of the sunflower, C. R. Lab. Carlsberg, Sér. chim. **23** (1940) 213

245) – – and Ida Smedley-MacLean, The synthesis of phospholipin in rats fed on the fat-deficient diet, Biochem. J. **34** (1940) 903

246) L. Hahn and – –, Rate of penetration of ions through the capillary wall, Acta Physiol. Scand. **1**, fasc. 3/4 (1941) 347

247) L. Hahn and – –, Potassium exchange in the stimulated muscle, Acta Physiol. Scand. **2**, fasc. 1 (1941) 51

248) – – and L. Hahn, Exchange of cellular potassium, Biol. Medd. Dan. Vid. Selsk. **16** (1941) No. 1

249) – –, L. Hahn and O. Rebbe, Circulation of phosphorus in the frog. With a note on the circulation of potassium, Biol. Medd. Dan. Vid. Selsk. **16** (1941) No. 8

250) – – and Niels Nielsen, Potassium interchange in yeast cells, Acta Physiol. Scand. **2**, fasc. 3/4 (1941) 347

251) Potassium interchange in the human body, Acta Physiol. Scand. **3**, fasc. 3 (1941) 123

252) Radioaktive Stoffer som Indikatorer i Biologien, Salmonsen Leksikon-Tidsskr. **9** (1941) 539

253) Jordens Alder, Nord. Astron. Tidsskr. (1942) No. 1

254) – – und H. v. Euler, Über die Permeabilität der Zellwand des Sarkoms für Phosphat und die Geschwindigkeit der Neubildung von phosphorhaltigen Verbindungen in den Sarkomzellen, Ark. Kemi, Miner., Geol. **15 A** (1942) No. 15

255) L. Hahn and – –, Rate of penetration of ions into erythrocytes, Acta Physiol. Scand. **3**, fasc. 3 (1942) 193

256) – – and K. Zerahn, Determination of the red corpuscle content, Acta Physiol. Scand. **4**, fasc. 3/4 (1942) 376

257) H. v. Euler und – –, Wirkung der Röntgenstrahlen auf den Umsatz der Nukleinsäure im Jensen-Sarkom, Biol. Medd. Dan. Vid. Selsk. **17** (1942) No. 8

258) Anvendelse af mærkede Atomer i Biologien, Naturens Verden **27** (1943) 193

259) – – and J. Ottesen, Rate of formation of nucleic acid in the organs of the rat, Acta Physiol. Scand. **5**, fasc. 2/3 (1943) 237

260) H. v. Euler und – –, Wirkung der Röntgenstrahlen auf den Umsatz der Nukleinsäure im Jensen-Sarkom. II, Ark. Kemi, Miner., Geol. **17A** (1943) No. 30

261) Retention of atoms of maternal origin in the adult white mouse, The Svedberg 1884-1944 (Stockholm 1944) 456

262) L. Ahlström, H. v. Euler und – –, Über die kurzlebige durch Röntgenstrahlen bewirkte Hemmung der Nukleinsäurebildung, Ark. Kemi, Miner., Geol. **18B** (1944) No. 13

263) – –, K. H. Köster, G. Sørensen, E. Warburg and K. Zerahn, The red corpuscle content of the circulating blood determined by labelling the erythrocytes with radio-phosphorus, Acta Med. Scand. **116**, fasc. 5/6 (1944) 561

264) Lucie Ahlström, Hans von Euler und – –, Die Wirkung von Röntgenstrahlen auf den Nukleinsäureumsatz in den Organen der Ratte, Ark. Kemi, Miner., Geol. **19A** (1944) No. 9

142

265) On the effect of Roentgen rays on cellular division, (Commemoration vol. for Niels Bohr's 60th birthday) Revs. Mod. Phys. **17** (1945) 102

266) Rate of renewal of the fish skeleton, Acta Phys. Scand. **9**, fasc. 3/4 (1945) 234

267) L. Ahlström, H. v. Euler und – –, Über die indirekte Wirkung von Röntgenstrahlen auf das Jensensarkom, Ark. Kemi, Miner., Geol. **19A** (1945) No. 13

268) Lucie Ahlström, Hans von Euler und – –, Bildung von Nukleinsäure in Sarkomschnitten, Ark. Kemi, Miner., Geol. **21A** (1945) No. 6

269) L. Ahlström, H. v. Euler, – – and K. Zerahn, Fate of the nucleic acid introduced into the circulation, Ark. Kemi, Miner., Geol. **22A** (1946) No. 7

270) Interaction between the phosphorus atoms of the wheat seedling and the nutrient solution, Ark. Bot. **33A** (1946) No. 2

271) Om isotopindikatorer, Suomen Kemistilehti **A19** (1946) 111; "Vetenskapen just nu" (1946) p. 559

272) E. Hammarsten and – –, Rate of renewal of ribo- and desoxyribo nucleic acids, Acta Physiol. Scand. **11**, fasc. 4 (1946) 335

273) Some applications of isotopic indicators. Nobel Lecture 1944, Les Prix Nobel en 1940-1944, (Stockholm 1946) p. 95
Reprinted in: Nobel Lectures Chemistry 1942-1962. (Elsevier Publ. Comp., Amsterdam 1964, p. 9)

274) C. Eklundh-Ehrenberg, H. v. Euler and – –, Note on the number of pollen grains identified in the fruit of the aspen, Ark. Kemi, Miner., Geol. **23B** (1946) No. 5

275) – – and K. Zerahn, The effect of Roentgen rays and ultraviolet radiation on the permeability of yeast, Acta Radiol. **27**, fasc. 3/4 (1946) 316

276) L. Ahlström, H. v. Euler, – – and K. Zerahn, Attempts to find products blocking nucleic acid formation in the circulation of an irradiated organism, Ark. Kemi, Miner., Geol. **23A** (1946) No. 10

277) H. v. Euler, U. S. v. Euler and – –, The effect of excitation on nerve permeability, Acta Physiol. Scand. **12**, fasc. 2/3 (1946) 261

278) Effect of X-rays on the rate of turnover of phosphatides, Nature **158** (1946) 268

279) L. Ahlström, H. v. Euler and – –, Turnover of nucleic acid in retrograde sarcomata, Ark. Kemi, Miner., Geol. **24A** (1947) No. 12

280) Effect of X-rays on phosphatide turnover, Ark. Kemi, Miner., Geol. **24A** (1947) No. 26

281) L. Ahlström, H. v. Euler and – –, Application of labelled substrates in the study of enzymic processes, Ark. Kemi, Miner., Geol. **24A** (1947) No. 27

282) Some applications of radioactive indicators in turnover studies, Advances in Enzymology **7** (1947) 111

283) Francis William Aston 1877-1945, Obituary Notices of Fellows of The Royal Society **5** (1948) 635; J. Chem. Soc. (1948) 1468

284) Preparation of radioactive tracers. Festskrift tillägnad J. Arvid Hedvall (Göteborg 1948) 249

285) H. v. Euler, – – and W. Solodkowska, Turnover of ribosenucleic acid in the Jensensarcoma of the rat, Ark. Kemi, Miner., Geol. **26A** (1948) No. 4

286) Radioactive Indicators. Their Application in Biochemistry, Animal Physiology and Pathology (Interscience Publ., New York 1948); First Russian Ed. (Moscow 1951); Second Russian Ed. (Moscow 1954)

287) Nucleic acid metabolism, Advances in Biol. and Med. Physics **1** (1948) 410

288) C. Elliot, L. Hahn and – –, Note on the inorganic phosphate of blood plasma, Acta Physiol. Scand. **16**, fasc. 1 (1948) 20

289) Conclusions générales. Echanges isotopiques et structure moléculaire (Coll. Intern. Paris 1948). J. Chim. Phys. **45** (1948) 249

290) Historical sketch of the biological application of tracer elements, Cold Spring Harbor Symposia on Quantitative Biology **13** (1949) 129

291) Effect of X-rays on the incorporation of carbon-14 into desoxyribonucleic acid, Nature **163** (1949) 869

143

292) Effect of X-rays on the incorporation of carbon-14 into animal tissue, Nature **164** (1949) 269

293) Exposé de l'historique des applications biologiques des indicateurs, Rc. Istituto Superiore di Sanità (Roma) **12** (1949) 637

294) Isotoper, Medicinska Framsteg (1949) 1

295) A great physical chemist, J. N. Brønsted Memorial Issue. Acta Chem. Scand. **3** (1949) 1205; The application of Brønsted's method of isotope separation to the study of the natural radio-activity of potassium, Ibid. **3** (1949) 1263

296) Effect of muscular exercise and of urethan administration on the incorporation of carbon-14 into animal tissue, Nature **164** (1949) 1007

297) Irma Andersson-Kottö and – –, Zinc uptake by neurospora, Biochem. J. **44** (1949) 407

298) Advances in medicine as a result of the use of isotopes, Sixth Intern. Congress of Pediatrics, Zürich (1950) (Transacts)

299) Grace de C. Elliot and – –, Turnover of phosphatides, Acta Physiol. Scand. **19**, fasc. 4 (1950) 370

300) Erinnerung an die alten Tage am Wiener Institut für Radiumforschung, Festschr. des Inst. f. Radiumforsch. anlässlich seines 40-jährigen Bestandes (1910-1950) Springer, Wien (1950) p. 47

301) The application of radioactive indicators in biochemistry, (Faraday Lecture) J. Chem. Soc. (1951) 1618

302) M. L. Beeckmans, H. Casier and – –, Effects of dinitrocyclo-pentylphenol on the incorporation of labelled acetate carbon ($C^{14}$) into tissue fractions, Arch. int. pharmacodyn. **86** (1951) 33

303) – –, R. Ruyssen and M. L. Beeckmans, Turnover rate of the fatty acids of the liver, Experientia **7/4** (1951) 144

304) – –, R. Ruyssen and M. L. Beeckmans, Effect of urethane on the incorporation of $C^{14}$ into animal tissue, Experientia **7/8** (1951) 317

305) Thorium B labelled red corpuscles, Ark. Kemi **3**, No. 46 (1951) 425

306) – – and A. Forssberg, Effect of irradiation by X-rays on the exhalation of carbon dioxide by the mouse, Nature **168** (1951) 692

307) – – and G. Nylin, Application of $^{42}K$ labelled red corpuscles in blood volume measurements, Acta Physiol. Scand. **24**, fasc. 4 (1951) 285

308) Historical notes on the discovery of hafnium, Ark. Kemi **3**, No. 58 (1951) 543

309) The application of radiocarbon in the study of radiolesions, J. Chim. Phys. **48** (1951) 275

310) – – and Gudrun Dreyfus, Effect of X-rays on the incorporation of $^{14}C$ into tissue fractions of the mouse, Ark. Kemi **4**, No. 22 (1952) 337

311) – –, Determination of the rate of renewal from the rate of disappearance of labelled molecules, Exp. Cell Res. **3** (1952) 192

312) Ionizing radiation and cellular metabolism. Symposium on Radiobiology, ed. James J. Nickson John Wiley and Sons, New York 1952, p. 189

313) Application of radioactive indicators in vascular studies, Symposium on Body Water, Edinburgh 1951; Advancement of Science **9** (1952) 57

314) A. Forssberg and – –, Effect of irradiation with X-rays on phosphate incorporation in mice, Ark. Kemi **5**, No. 11 (1952) 93

315) Über die Anwendung von radioaktiven Indikatoren. 2. Tagung der Nobelpreisträger in Lindau, Juni 1952. Chimia **6** (1962) 201

316) Some historical remarks on the application of radioactive indicators (Dedicated to Professor Gustav Nylin on his 60th Birthday) Cardiologia **21**, fasc. 4/5 (1952) 226

317) Effect of irradiation with X-rays on the catabolism of methylalcohol in the mouse, Acta Physiol. Scand. **30**, fasc. 1 (1953) 90

318) Radioaktive Indikatoren in Medizin und Naturwissenschaft, Naturw. Rundschau, Heft 6 (1953) 221

319) – – and Gustav Nylin, Application of "Thorium B" labeled red corpuscles in blood volume studies, Circulation Res. **1** (1953) 102

320) Foreword to G. E. Francis, W. Mulligan and A. Wormall, "Isotopic Tracers" (London 1954)

144

321) Application of radioactive isotopes as indicators in radiobiology. 7th Intern. Congr. Radiology, Acta Radiologia, Suppl. 116 (1954) 423

322) Die Anwendung der radioaktiven Indikatoren in der Radiobiologie, Strahlentherapie 93 (1954) 325

323) K. Agner, R. Bonnichsen and – –, Note on the determination of radioiron, Scand. J. Clin. Lab. Invest. 6 (1954) 261

324) Über biochemische Wirkungen ionisierender Strahlen, Naturw. Rundschau 7, Heft 2 (1954) 45

325) A. Forssberg and – –, Effect of X-rays on the resorption rate of injected $NaH^{14}CO_3$ in mice, Third Radiobiol. Conf. Liège (1954) p. 148

326) – – and G. Dal Santo, Effect of adrenaline on the interaction between plasma and tissue constituents, Acta Physiol. Scand. 32, fasc. 4 (1954) 339

327) K. Agner, R. Bonnichsen and – –, Distribution in rabbit livers of intravenously injected iron (Abstract), Acta Chem. Scand. 8 (1954) 1104

328) Conservation of skeletal calcium atoms through life, Biol. Medd. Dan. Vid. Selsk. 22 (1955) No. 9

329) R. Bonnichsen, – – and Å. Åkeson, Formation of radiosensitivity of myoglobin, Nature 175 (1955) 723

330) Effect of irradiation with X-rays on the catabolism of ethylalcohol in the mouse, Acta Physiol. Scand. 33, fasc. 2/3 (1955) 238

331) R. Bonnichsen and – –, Effect of irradiation on hemin formation, Acta Chem. Scand. 9 (1955) 509

332) R. Bonnichsen, – – and Å. Åkeson, Formation of myoglobin, Acta Physiol. Scand. 34, fasc. 4 (1955) 345

333) Arne Forssberg and – –, Note on the effect of X-rays and hormones on the resorption rate of injected $NaH^{14}CO_3$, Acta Physiol. Scand. 35, fasc. 1 (1955) 84; Effect of X-rays and hormones on resorption rate of injected $NaH^{14}CO_3$, Amer. J. Physiol. 180 (1955) 325

334) – – and R. Bonnichsen, Some aspects on the effect of irradiation with Röntgen rays on hemoglobin formation, Annales Acad. Scient. Fenn. Ser. A, 2 Chemica (1955) 60, 295 ("Biochemistry of Nitrogen", A. I. Virtanen homage volume)

335) Radioactive tracers and their application. Intern. Conf. On the Peaceful Use of Atomic Energy, Geneva. Proc. 16 (1955) 75

336) Der Kreislauf des Eisens im Tierkörper, Naturw. Rundschau 8, Heft 10 (1955) 380

337) Isotope als Indikatoren in der physiologischen Forschung, Documenta Rheumatologica Geigy, No. 6 (Basel 1955) p. 5

338) Anwendung von Isotop-Indikatoren in der Hämatologie, 5. Kongr. Europ. Ges. Hämatologie, Freiburg 1955. (Springer, Berlin 1956, p. 10)

339) Der Weg der Atome durch die Generationen, Naturw. Rundschau 9, Heft 6 (1956) 212

340) Om radioaktiva isotoper och deras användning. "Sverige inför Atomåldern" (Bonnier, Stockholm 1956) 173

341) Radioactive tracers in radiobiological studies (36th Silvanus Thompson Memorial Lecture), Brit. J. Radiol. 29 (1956) 465

342) G. Häggqvist und – –, Morphologische Untersuchungen über die Wirkungen des schweren Wassers, Acta Morphol. Neerlando-Scand. 1 (1956) 1

343) – – and A. Forssberg, Biochemical effects produced by ionizing radiation. Third Intern. Congr. Biochemistry, Brussels 1955. Ed. C. Liébecq. Academic Press Inc., New York 1956, p. 479

344) G. v. Ehrenstein and – –, Embryonal iron turnover, Acta Physiol. Scand. 38, fasc. 2 (1956) 184

345) Path of atoms through generations, The Scientific Monthly 83 (1956) 238; Universitas 2 (1958) 51

346) G. Häggqvist und – –, Morphologische Veränderungen bei Mäusen nach Einnahme von schwerem Wasser ($D_2O$), "Verh. Dtsch. Zool. Ges. Hamburg 1956", Akadem. Verlagsges., Leipzig (1956); Zool. Anzeiger, suppl. 20 (1956) 130

145

347) Les indicateurs radioactifs dans la recherche radiobiologique, "Protection contre les Radiations Ionisantes" CEN Saclay (Ecole Nat. de la Santé Publique) No. 22 (1956) 16

348) Fragor av betydelse för cancerforskningen behandlade vid 5'te intern. radiobiologikonf., Cancer 2 (1956) 12

349) Therapeutic use of artificial radioisotopes. "The Therapeutic Radiation Problem" (Introduction) ed. P. Hahn (Wiley Sons, New York 1956, p. 1

350) Glykosmetabolismen efter röntgenbestrålning, Riksföreningen för kräftsjukdomarnas bekämpande, Årsb. 1, 1952-1956 (Stockholm 1957) 76

351) R. Bonnichsen, G. Ehrenstein, – – and J. Schliack, Haemoglobin present in the nuclear fraction of the liver, Acta Chem. Scand. 11 (1957) 120

352) Renewal of the mineral constituents of the skeleton, Intern. J. Appl. Radiation and Isotopes 2 (1957) 85

353) Die Bedeutung der Radio-Isotopen-Forschung für Medizin und Biologie, Strahlentherapie 102 (1957) 341

354) Note on the chloride content of the mineral constituents of the skeleton, Acta Chem. Scand. 11 (1957) 261

355) Historical progress of the isotopic methodology and its influences on the biological sciences, Minerva Nucleare 1 (1957) 189

356) Fritz Paneth 70 Jahre, Physikal. Blätter 13 (1957) 414

357) Anwendung von Isotopindikatoren in physiologischen Untersuchungen, Klin. Wschr. 35 (1957) 201

358) Gedenkworte für Heinrich Wieland 1877-1957, Ordre Pour Le Mérite für Wissenschaften und Künste, Reden und Gedenkworte 3 (1958) 13

359) G. Häggqvist and – –, The combined effect of heavy water and Roentgen irradiation on the animal organism, Acta Radiol. 49 (1958) 321

360) Die Krebsanämie, Naturw. Rundschau 11, Heft 7 (1958) 247

361) Geleitwort zu E. Broda: Radioaktive Isotope in der Biologie (Deuticke, Wien 1958)

362) A scientific career, Perspectives in Biology and Medicine 1 (1958) 345

363) Einige Anwendungen des radioaktiven Eisens. In "Beiträge zur Physik und Chemie des 20. Jahrhunderts" (Vieweg und Sohn, Braunschweig, 1959) 115

364) Günter v. Ehrenstein and – –, The physiological iron loss by the mouse, Acta Haemat. 22 (1959) 311

365) Radioaktive Markierung von Zellen, Naturw. Rundschau 12, Heft 9 (1959) 325

366) Hematopoesen vid cancer. Riksföreningen mot Cancer, Årsb. 2, 1957-59. (Stockholm 1960) 232

367) Radioaktive Markierung von Zellen. Bibl. "Nutritio et Dieta" 1, fasc. 1 (1960) 178

368) – – and H.-L. Kottmeier, Turnover of plasma iron in cancer patients prior to and after treatment, Acta Obst. et Gynec. Scandinav. 39 (1960) 675.

369) Åke Åkeson, G. v. Ehrenstein, – – and Hugo Theorell, Life span of myoglobin, Arch. Biochem. Biophys. 91 (1960) 310

370) Einige Anwendungen von Isotopindikatoren in der Physiologie, Pflügers Archiv 272 (1961) 195

371) Marie Curie and her contemporaries. (The Becquerel-Curie Memorial Lecture: Eighth Annual Meeting, The Society of Nuclear Medicine, Pittsburgh 1961), J. Nuclear Med. 2 (1961) 169

372) A. Forssberg, G. Dreyfus and – –, The labelling of nucleic acids in tissue cells, Ark. Kemi 18, No. 11 (1961) 173

373) – – und Arne Forssberg, Über die atomare Stabilität der Desoxyribonukleinsäure-Moleküle, Strahlentherapie 116 (1961) 324

374) Historische Übersicht der Anwendung von Isotopindikatoren. In "Künstliche radioaktive Isotope in Physiologie, Diagnostik und Therapie", ed. H. Schwieck und F. Turba, 2. Aufl., Springer-Verlag, Berlin 1961, p. 536
Einige allgemeine Bemerkungen über die Anwendung von Isotopindikatoren, Ibid. p. 591

375) Adventures in radioisotope research. 2 vols. (Pergamon Press, London 1962)

146

376) – – and D. Lockner, Iron metabolism in health and in the neoplastic state, Ark. Kemi **19**, No. 26 (1962) 303

377) Iron metabolism in normal and tumor-bearing mice. In "On Cancer and Hormones" (Univ. of Chicago Press 1962) 141

378) Historische Übersicht über einige Anwendungen radioaktiver Isotope in der Hämatologie. In "Radio-Isotope in der Hämatologie". I. Intern. Symposium, Freiburg 1962. Herausg. W. Keiderling und G. Hoffmann. Friedrich-Karl Schattauer-Verlag, Stuttgart 1962. Nuclear-Medizin Suppl. 1 ad **2** (1962) 1

379) Historical notes to the discovery of the cosmic radiation, Pontif. Acad. Scient., Commentari **1** No. 21 (1962) 1

380) Der Umsatz des Plasmaeisens und seine klinische Bedeutung;
Le métabolisme du fer plasmatique et son importance en clinique Triangel (Sandoz) **5**, No. 6 (1962) 260

381) Iron transport rate in the neoplastic organism, Pontif. Acad. Scient., Scripta Varia No. 22 (1962) 1

382) Järnets fördelning i den normala och i den neoplastiska organismen. Riksföreningen mot cancer, Årsb. **3**, 1960-62 (Stockholm 1962), 212

383) Gamle dage. In "Niels Bohr, Et Mindeskrift", Fysisk Tidsskr. **60** (1963) 26

384) D. Lockner, K. Sletten and – –, Studies on cancer anaemia, Organ weights, blood values and iron metabolism in normal and tumour-bearing mice, Brit. J. Cancer **17** (1963) 328

385) Life span of tissue cells, Acta Chem. Scand. **17**, Suppl. 1 (1963) 17

386) Der Weg der Atome durch die Generationen, Universitas **18** (1963) 257

387) Die Radioaktivität als Hilfsmittel der Forschung, In "Strahlenschutz in Forschung und Praxis" **3**, p. 9 (Rombach, Freiburg/Br. 1963)

388) – –, D. Lockner and K. Sletten, Iron metabolism and erythrocyte formation in fish, Acta physiol. scand **60** (1964) 256

389) Diurnale Variation biologischer Vorgänge, Ark. Kemi **23**, No. 6 (1964) 57

390) – –, Dieter Lockner und Ulf Eriksson, Die Wirkung von Strahlen auf die Lebensdauer der Erythrocyten von Tumormäusen, Arzneim.-Forsch. (Drug Res.) **14** (1964) 741

391) – –, D. Lockner und K. Sletten, Über die Strahlensensibilität extramedullarer Hämopoese, Med. Welt No. 10 (1964) 455

392) K. Sletten, D. Lockner and – –, Radiosensitivity of haemopoiesis in fish. I. Studies at 18°C, Intern. J. Rad. Biol. **8** (1964) 317

393) Isotopic measurements on the life-cycle of tissue cells. In "Isotopic and Cosmic Chemistry", Dedicated to Harold C. Urey on his seventieth birthday, April 29, 1963. (North-Holland Publ. Comp., Amsterdam 1964) 34

394) Dieter Lockner, Ulf Ericson and – –, Copper turnover in blood plasma, Acta haemat. **33** (1965) 1

395) D. Lockner, U. Ericson and – –, Haematological effects of ionizing radiation in cancerous mice, Intern. J. Rad. Biol. **9** (1965) 143

396) The historical background of some applications of isotopic tracers in analytical chemistry. In "Radiochemical Methods of Analysis" **1** (1965) 3 (Intern. Atomic Energy Agency, Vienna)

397) Selected papers of George Hevesy (Pergamon Press, London, in print)

268a) – – and J. Ottesen, Life cycle of the red corpuscles of the hen, Nature **156** (1945) 534.